COUNTRY WINES

Making and Using Wines from Herbs, Fruits, Flowers, and More

Pattie Vargas and Rich Gulling

A Garden Way Publishing Book

STOREY

Storey Communications, Inc.
Schoolhouse Road
Pownal, Vermont 05261

Cover and text design by Andrea Gray
Cover photograph by Nicholas Whitman
Edited by Jill Mason
Interior line drawings by Elayne Sears
Indexed by Joyce Goldenstern

The name Garden Way Publishing is licensed to Storey Communications, Inc., by Garden Way, Inc.

Printed in the United States by Capital City Press
First Printing, December 1991

Library of Congress Cataloging-in-Publication Data

Vargas, Pattie, 1941-
    Country wines : making & using wines from herbs, fruits, flowers & more / by Pattie Vargas & Rich Gulling.
        p.   cm.
    "A Garden Way Publishing book."
    Includes index.
    ISBN 0-88266-749-1 (pb)
    1. Fruit wines.   I. Gulling, Rich, 1961-   II. Title.
TP561.V37   1992
641.2'29—dc20
                          91-746
                          CIP

For Ida Winans, who taught us how to value those things we create for ourselves and the joy of sharing them with others.

Contents

Introduction

*L*earning about winemaking can be a lifelong process for the connoisseur, but most of us don't aspire to be master vintners. We may just want to make a little "bottled sunshine," as Ray Bradbury so aptly described dandelion wine, or we may have too many berries and no place to store them. We may simply want the fun of creating a memory and a legacy for our children to remember as part of the "good old days." This book is for the novice. The recipes can be made without a lot of technical knowledge or fancy equipment and will produce *delicious* wines. While there are a number of books devoted to making, storing, tasting, smelling, and even investing in vintage wines, this book will give you a basic knowledge of the processes that occur when you make country wines.

Although the classical definition of wine is "the product of the fermentation of grapes," it's easy to make a case for dividing wine into two major categories: wines made with grapes as the main ingredient, and country wines made from fruits, herbs, nuts, and even flowers and vegetables, and seasoned with the creativity and imagination of amateur winemakers through generations. In this book, we refer to both as wine, but beware of the connoisseur who thinks your "bottled sunshine" is not really wine at all. A glass of well-made country wine will go a long way toward softening that position.

The legal requirements involved with winemaking have been simplified in recent years so that no registration with the Bureau of Alcohol, Tobacco and Firearms needs to be made in order to make wine in your home. However, the ATF does impose two restrictions on home winemakers: First, none of the wine produced for personal consumption may in any way be sold or bartered. Second, a family may produce no more than two hundred gallons of wine for personal use each year; that amount is reduced to one hundred gallons for a single head of household. As long as these requirements are met, the home winemaker needn't worry about breaking the law.

Although winemaking is a patient process, the beginner will probably want to get right to it. We hope this book will be the first step toward a rewarding and pleasurable pastime.

1

Winemaking Made Easy

Although America's old-time country winemakers drew on a winemaking tradition that may date back to 3000 B.C., when grapes are believed to have originated in southern Russia, they probably relied on observation and hand-me-down recipes rather than scientific techniques to create a wide variety of delectable homemade beverages. In fact, with the kind of reverse snobbery that often characterized the frontier's pioneers, they undoubtedly thought wines made from European grapes were "high falutin'."

But country wines do have a tradition of their own — a tradition as sophisticated as Dom Perignon's scientific blending of flavors or as simple as a serf's sunny mead created in a thatched kitchen. Some country-wine recipes undoubtedly accompanied immigrants to America from many different countries; old-country traditions were adapted to whichever fruits or flowers were plentiful in the Kentucky hills or on the Nebraska plains. Other recipes came from the imaginations of pioneers who approached winemaking at its simplest level: mix fruit juices, sugar, and yeast; allow the mixture to ferment away from the air; wait patiently. In a few months, a new wine would be ready for tasting.

If those first sips brought smiles, a tradition was born. If not, the recipe was altered to make the wine more or less acid or more or less sweet until the winemaker — and his friends and neighbors — was satisfied.

Those country wines fermented with no special equipment. A crock, a plate, and a handful of dried beans to hold down the plate put Great-grandpa in the winemaking business. He probably nicked a little of Grandma's bread yeast to get the fermentation process started and then waited patiently for nature to take its course. If his wine was cloudy after repeated syphoning and straining over several months' time, he added a dried eggshell or two to clear the mixture. He syphoned the liquid into jugs or bottles a few days later, driving the cork home with a block of wood and a hammer.

If your interest in country winemaking is more historical than epicurean, you can use these ancestral methods with all the recipes in this book. You won't need much in the way of special equipment, and most of the time you'll end up with acceptable country wines. But old-time methods produced their share of failures, too. As we searched out old recipes, tested them, tasted them, and, in the tradition of country winemakers everywhere, adapted them to suit our tastes, we opted for a few — just a few — of the modern tools and techniques that ensure well-made country wines every time. We'll tell you about both methods. Then you can decide which way you'll wet your whistle.

WINES LIKE GRANDPA USED TO MAKE

The first wine we ever made was from a backyard grapevine. The grapes were Concords, and, since nobody in our family liked Concord grapes, we decided to make them into wine. Our only problem was that we knew next to nothing about making wine. We crushed the grapes, filtered off the juice, poured the juice into a wine carafe with a cut-glass stopper, put the carafe into a cupboard, and forgot about it. Some months later we rediscovered the carafe. Sediment had formed in the bottom, but the liquid above it was clear and sparkling.

Inadvertently, we had provided the only conditions necessary to turn grape juice into wine. Wild yeasts were already present on the grape skins when we crushed the grapes, and the grapes themselves provided sugar, acid, flavor, and tannins. The cut-glass stopper prevented additional air from entering the carafe, but allowed carbon dioxide to be released. When carbon dioxide (a fermentation by-product) built up inside, the pressure caused the stopper to rise, emit a "burp" of CO_2, and fall back into place, shutting out the outside air.

Since that time, we've learned a lot about making wine, but the first batches we made were all experiments, and the equipment we used was whatever we had around the house. It consisted of a new plastic wastebasket, scrubbed and sterilized diligently each time we used it, a couple of gallon-size, wide-mouth, glass fruit jars, a strainer, some rubber tubing, and some recycled wine bottles.

The First Fermentation

We made wine much the same as our ancestors did. We put the ingredients in the wastebasket for the first fermentation, stirring them once or twice a day, and covered the basket with foil in between times. (Grandpa probably used a stoneware crock and covered it with a clean cloth. He would have told you that keeping the mixture loosely covered is essential to keep out those tiny flies that will turn your wine to vinegar — and he would have been right. Fruit or vinegar flies seem to appear by magic around fermenting fruit, and they carry bacteria that can easily turn wine to vinegar.)

This first fermentation takes place in the presence of air and is sometimes quite energetic, so you need a container that's large enough to allow the mixture to ferment without bubbling over. Since all the recipes in this book make wine in the amount of 1 gallon, we recommend a 2-gallon (or larger) plastic container for this first fermentation. You may want to fill a 1-gallon container with water, dump it into the 2-gallon one, and mark the level on the outside for reference — many of our recipes call for adding "enough water to make a gallon." Some recipes will require more than one of each container.

In our early experiments, we found that the first vigorous fermentation slowed down after a few days, and we syphoned the juice into the glass jars. We learned that winemakers call this process *racking*; it involves using a piece of rubber or plastic tubing to syphon the juice into a clean container while leaving the solids in the fermentation vat — in our case, the plastic wastebasket. The mixture of juice and solids is called the *must*, but once you've finished separating the two, the slightly cloudy liquid you've racked into a clean crock, jug, or jar is wine — even though it has a way to go before you'll want to serve it with fine food and candlelight.

Sometimes a *cap* forms on the top of the must, composed of solids that, instead of sinking to the bottom of the container, float to the top. If this cap is too dense, it can prevent oxygen from getting to the growing yeast cells in the wine during the aerobic phase of the fermentation process. So you'll need to punch a hole in the cap to allow oxygen through; otherwise, the yeast could stop growing and cause a *stuck fermentation* (see Glossary, page 164). You'll need to be careful, though, not to stir all that stuff back into the wine, because the wine will take longer to clear if you do, even with careful racking.

Racking is really very simple. Just place the tubing into the must and start the syphoning action by sucking on the free end of the

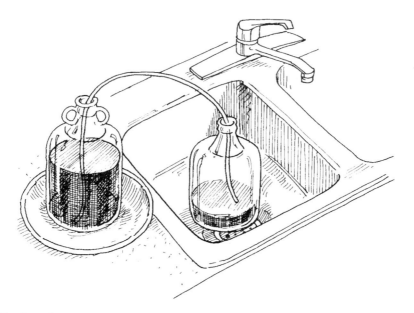

Placing the container into which you're racking the wine in the sink avoids the problem of messy spills.

tube, much as you would a soda straw. Be sure that the end of the tube is at least an inch above the sediment in the bottom. When the wine starts to flow, tuck the end of the tube into a clean container that's positioned a little lower than the original container. (See page 151 for more.) The wine will continue to flow downward until all of the liquid is transferred to the second fermentation vessel. If a cap has formed on the top of the must, carefully insert the syphon tube through the cap, and the cleared wine underneath will flow out, leaving both the bottom sediment (the *lees*) and the cap to be discarded.

During our early research, one country winemaker told us she always knew when it was time to rack the wine from the first fermentation because the mixture stopped "whispering," the sound made by the escaping carbon dioxide during the first, vigorous fermentation.

The Second Fermentation

Once we racked the wine into the gallon jars, it was ready for the second fermentation. This fermentation is much less vigorous than the first one, so we filled the jars almost to the rim. But the second fermentation differs from the first one in another important way. For the yeast to produce alcohol most efficiently, it needs to grow and reproduce without oxygen. That meant that we needed to devise a way to keep air out of the jars while the wine fermented — a way that would also allow the carbon dioxide to be released. Putting on a tight lid at this point would result in an exploding jar once the carbon-dioxide pressure built up to a critical level. So we needed a device that would let the carbon dioxide out while keeping oxygen from getting into the jar.

We opted for the same kind of primitive fermentation lock that early winemakers used. We covered each jar mouth with a luncheon plate and weighted it down with a handful of dried beans. When the carbon-dioxide pressure built to the point that it could lift the plate, a small burp of carbon dioxide escaped and the plate settled back into place. The plate and the continuing positive pressure in the jar kept the air outside as the wine continued its slow second fermentation.

Old-time winemakers covered a crock with a plate and weighted it down with a handful of dried beans.

Different kinds of country wines require different numbers of rackings and fermentations before they're completely clear. Just keep an eye on your jars, and when you are satisfied that the wine is clear enough to sparkle in your best wineglasses, it's ready to bottle.

Bottling the Wine

Home winemakers often use a variety of containers to store wine, but we seldom take the chance of having ill-fitting corks or inadvertent contamination that can occur when you use non-standard containers. Wine bottles aren't really expensive if you consider that you can use them over and over again as long as you make sure to keep them clean and sterilize them before reusing them. In this age of recycling, you can probably find a bar or restaurant that will save wine bottles for you, provided you don't live in a state where reusing commercial wine bottles is prohibited by law. We almost always reuse the bottles from wines that we make or buy.

Wine bottles come in a variety of shapes — traditionally related to the region where the wine was produced or the kind of wine the bottles contain, such as Burgundy, claret, Rhine wine, or champagne — but the amount of wine the bottle holds is pretty standard. Most winemakers, or wine buyers, for that matter, assume that the standard bottle, holding approximately 25 ounces, is what is meant

Left to right: Bottles of Rhine wine, claret, Burgundy, and champagne.

by a *bottle* of wine. True, some wines are sold in half-gallon or gallon containers, but these wines are usually designated as *jug wines*.

Some winemakers use caps to seal their wine bottles, but we don't recommend it. Traditionally, fine wines are corked and stored in a rack that keeps the bottles on their sides with the necks slightly lower than the bottoms. That position keeps the corks moistened with wine so they swell and form a tight seal. Screw-on caps may allow some air leakage, and caps applied with a bottle-capper are more appropriate to beer or soda pop than to wine. We recommend using standard wine bottles and sterile corks — brand

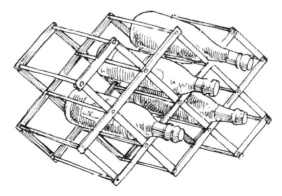

Storing wine on its side with the neck of the bottle slightly lower than the bottom keeps the cork moist and tight.

new or scalded or sterilized chemically (see page 138). If you do use screw-on caps, dipping the necks of the bottles into melted paraffin may keep the seal tighter, but you'll need to be careful to avoid bumping the wax coating and breaking the seal.

Be sure that fermentation is complete before you cork the bottles tightly. Otherwise, your impatience might be rewarded with exploding bottles, flying glass, and a messy clean-up job. We are usually careful to put the cork only one-fourth of the way into the bottle for a week or two. Then, if the wine isn't quite finished, we'll have a few popping corks but no broken bottles. If cork-popping becomes too vigorous, the wine probably needs to be returned to an airlocked vessel for another month or so. (See page 151.)

Since wine improves with age, it should always be *cellared*, stored for a period of time, before it is sampled. Various recipes specify different lengths of time, depending on the kind of wine. Winemakers probably say "cellar the wine" instead of "store the wine in a cool, dark place" because it's shorter and pretty descriptive of the kinds of conditions that are best for long-term storage. Be sure to label each bottle before you store it.

If you are interested in making country wines the way our great-grandparents did it, the method we have described will work for any of the recipes in this book. You can use it on a small scale and probably be happy with the results most of the time. But if you want consistently good wine, we strongly suggest that you take advantage of some of the modern winemaking supplies we have incorporated into our still-simple system of making wine.

OLD WINES WITH A NEW TWIST

Winemaking Equipment

If you'd like a little insurance that your wines won't spoil, develop off-flavors, or turn to vinegar, you'll probably want to obtain a couple of pieces of the equipment that's available either in stores that sell winemaking equipment and supplies or through numerous mail-order catalogs. (We've listed some mail-order suppliers in the back of this book, page 166.)

Two items that top the list of useful winemaking equipment: a collapsible plastic fermentation vessel and some examples of fermentation locks.

Our favorite winemaking accessories are collapsible fermentation vessels made of white or clear plastic (rather like that used in plastic milk jugs) and fermentation locks that fit easily into the necks of these containers. The vessels are lightweight and portable, and the locks solve the problem of venting carbon dioxide while they keep air from getting inside. Our first fermentations still take place in plastic buckets or wastebaskets that are large enough to keep the must from bubbling over when the fermentation is especially vigorous, but these two items make subsequent fermentations much more manageable. Both are easily cleaned and relatively inexpensive.

Winemaking Supplies

Most old-time country-wine recipes use bread yeast to get the fermentation started, and some good wines have been made that way. But as we experimented with making wines, we also made

Equipment and supplies used in making country wines at home.

some batches with *commercial wine yeasts*, and those wines were always superior. First, the taste was better because wine yeasts come in a number of different varieties for different kinds of wines. That lets you pick a yeast that suits the kind of wine you're making — a port yeast for a deep red wine, for example. Commercial wine yeasts also give you a firmer sediment, and that makes racking easier and more efficient.

Particularly with honey wines (tastiest made with a champagne yeast), but also with wines made from certain high-pectin fruits, clarity is a problem even after diligent racking. A little research showed us that this cloudiness probably results from too much *pectin* — the same substance that turns fruit juice into jelly. Although murky wine won't hurt you, it isn't as pretty as we like our wines to be. Adding *pectic enzyme* to these wines when we make them solves the problem; the enzyme digests the pectin that keeps the wine from clearing.

Honey wines present another problem, as well. The combinations of ingredients in many honey wines simply do not have the nutrients necessary to complete the fermentation process. Old-timers used to add citrus juices to their must to provide these nutrients as well as the acid component that gives wines their character. (Any fruit pulp provides nutrients, but most winemakers add citrus fruits to wine recipes because they affect the flavor of the wine the least, adding mostly acid instead of the stronger flavors that other fruits contribute.) But adding a commercial *yeast nutrient* — a kind of vitamin pill for wine — and a commercial *acid blend* is more convenient and ensures that yeast grows efficiently and produces wine that's acid enough for best flavor. Since yeast nutrient and acid blend are natural products that work during the fermentation process, we feel comfortable adding them to our wines as needed. Yeast nutrient is included in all our recipes just to make sure that all the necessary nutrients are present, even in recipes calling for citrus. In wines without citrus or other acid fruits, we also add the acid blend.

If you are going to be incurring the slight additional cost of specialty wine yeasts, you may want to make sure that your purchased yeast is the only yeast to flavor your wine. Otherwise, you're taking the chance that some wild yeasts already present on the fruit or equipment will add unwanted flavors. Experienced winemakers are careful to eliminate that possibility. Even if you are willing to make wine as Grandma and Grandpa did, cleanliness in every aspect of the winemaking process is extremely important. Old-time country winemakers had to take their chances with yeasts, but the good ones took great care to see that their equipment was squeaky clean — preferably sterile. Bacteria that cause spoilage or turn wine to vinegar always lurk in the background. Boiling and scalding of everything used in the old-timers' winemaking endeavours greatly improved the taste and keeping quality of their wines.

Today, most winemakers rely on easier methods. If you prefer to use at-hand materials, a tablespoon of household chlorine bleach in a gallon of water will serve to keep your equipment free of bacteria and wild yeasts. If you use it, be sure to rinse, rinse, rinse. Obviously, you don't want to taste bleach in your wine. By far the easiest way to keep everything free of wild yeasts and bacteria is to use *Campden tablets*. They eliminate wild yeasts and bacteria from winemaking equipment by releasing sulfur dioxide gas when you dissolve them in water (1 crushed tablet per gallon). You can immerse fermentation locks and tubing in the solution just before using them. When you add a Campden tablet to your must, you'll eliminate all bacteria and yeast from it, but the effect lasts for just 24 hours. After that time elapses, you can add a prepared yeast culture and your wine will be bubbling in no time. Many winemakers let ingredients sit for 24 hours, well covered, before adding yeast to the must so that flavors permeate the juices even if they don't use Campden tablets. Although they are always optional, you may use Campden tablets with any recipe in this book.

Another ingredient that you'll find listed in some of our recipes is *tannin*, or grape tannin. A component of the skins and stems of some fruits — especially red fruits like grapes, plums, apples, and elderberries — tannins do a number of nice things to your wine. First of all, they give wine a certain zip by creating a hint of dryness in the mouth when you drink it. Without tannins, wine becomes a ho-hum beverage, common as soda pop. Equally important, tannins improve a wine's keeping qualities.

So in country-wine recipes that are likely to be short on tannins — wines made from flowers, herbs, grains, or vegetables — we add them. This need for tannins is one of the reasons that so many country-wine recipes call for raisins — dried grapes that retain tannins on their skins. Old-time winemakers may not have known why raisins made their wines taste better, but they knew that they did. And there are other ways to add tannins to your wines. A tablespoon of strong tea or even a couple of oak leaves added to the must gives added zest to recipes that you've found a bit dull. Or you can add commercial tannins, available from winemaking suppliers. (See list on page 166.)

A New Twist on Methods

Most old country-wine recipes use pretty much the same methods of preparation — crushing fruit, adding sugar or honey, and adding yeast, either by spreading cake yeast on a slice of bread and floating it on top of the must or by sprinkling dry yeast into the must mixture. Once the yeast is in the must, it begins to grow, but sometimes it takes several days for it to multiply enough to start a vigorous first fermentation. You can speed up this process by using a *yeast starter-culture* in your wines. Aside from the satisfaction of being able to speed up *anything* in the winemaking process, we think a vigorous fermentation that begins immediately results in a fresher-tasting wine. (Always be sure to let the wine ingredients cool before adding the yeast starter-culture; too much heat will kill the wine yeasts.)

Essentially, a yeast starter-culture is made by inoculating a small quantity of fruit juice with wine yeast (and yeast nutrients) so that the yeast begins to multiply rapidly. When you add this starter-culture to your wine, it is already filled with growing yeast cells so fermentation is more efficient. It's simple. Just add a package of wine yeast (5–7 grams) and a teaspoon of yeast nutrient to 1H cups of tepid fruit juice in a small, sterilized container. Cover, shake vigorously, and let stand at room temperature for a few hours (1–3 hours) until it gets bubbly. Orange juice makes an all-purpose starter-culture, because the orange flavor is mild enough that you can use it in any kind of wine without affecting the final flavor, so we generally use that. But you may substitute an equal amount of juice from the fruit you're using in your wine if you prefer.

If you increase the ingredients in your wine recipe to make a larger amount of wine — say, five gallons instead of one — you do not have to add additional starter-culture. The yeast in your wine is alive and growing, and it will continue to grow in the must until it has converted the sugar to the maximum concentration of alcohol that a given yeast will tolerate. Once the alcohol content reaches that point, fermentation will stop and whatever sugar remains in the solution gives the wine its sweetness. Dry wines have little sugar remaining in them; sweet ones have more. (If you prefer a sweeter wine than the one you've made, all you need to do is add more sugar than the recipe calls for in your next batch. You can even add more sugar to a finished wine, but doing so may cause an additional fermentation if the maximum alcohol content hasn't been reached. In that case, return the wine to an airlocked vessel and wait until it stops fermenting before you re-bottle. Remember, though, that a little sugar goes a long way in a finished wine. Add only small amounts and taste frequently so you don't overdo it.)

A Word about Preservatives

Old-time country winemakers usually made wines in small quantities and seldom kept them for longer than a year or two. For that reason, you'll seldom find country wines that contain much in the way of preservatives. If our grandparents wanted to keep wines over a longer period, they often added additional alcohol for greater preservative action — a process called *fortifying* a wine. But you can also stabilize your wines if you want to keep them for long periods of time by adding 1 crushed Campden tablet per gallon of finished wine (even if you already added one to the must).

Adding sulfur dioxide through the use of Campden tablets gives you control of the kind of yeasts in your wine and imparts better keeping qualities, but you do need to be aware that some sulfites will remain in the wine — about fifty parts per million — just in case you're one of those folks whose nose gets stuffy after drinking wine. Even a very small amount is enough to cause an allergic reaction in a sensitive person. Almost all commercial wines have sulfites as a preservative, but after sulfites received a lot of bad press a few years ago, commercial winemakers began to include a "contains sulfites" warning on their labels to protect the small number of people who are allergic to them. Be sure to let your guests know if your wines have sulfites — in very rare cases sulfite allergies cause dangerous or deadly reactions.

2

Wines from Native Fruits

*L*ining up bottles of colorful homemade wines in your cellar or pantry is especially rewarding if you've harvested the fruit from your own berry patch or fruit orchard. The wines in this chapter have the homey charm of sparkling homemade jams and jellies and fresh-baked fruit pies. But they endure over time so that years down the road you can sample a bottle and remember the summer when the apples almost broke the boughs in your orchard and the berries were so bursting with juice that it ran down your chin when you bit into one. And save some for when your children are grown so they can taste the summers of their youth. Surely that will be a treasure that few can share!

DRY APPLE WINE

Apple wines delighted our ancestors because they represented an economical way to preserve the abundance of fruit that a standard apple tree usually produced. After the jellies were sparkling on the pantry shelf beside the apple butter, after dried apples were stored away and the root cellar was stocked with baskets of the best fresh apples for storage, after the smaller ones were sauced and cidered, there were still enough left for Grandpa to make up some batches of apple wine — and that delightful beverage was just coming into its own when most of the other preserved apples had disappeared from the family stores.

1 teaspoon pectic enzyme
5 pints apple juice (without preservatives)
2½ pounds sugar
1 tablespoon citric acid *or* 2 ounces acid blend
1 Campden tablet (optional)
1 package wine yeast (5–7 grams)
1 teaspoon yeast nutrient
1½ cups apple juice

Add the pectic enzyme to the apple juice in a 2-gallon plastic bucket or wastebasket. Then add the sugar and citric acid and enough water to make 1 gallon. Add a Campden tablet to the must, if desired, and let the mixture stand, well covered, for 24 hours before proceeding. Make a yeast starter-culture by combining the wine yeast and yeast nutrient with 1½ cups tepid apple juice. Cover, shake vigorously, and let stand until bubbly (1–3 hours); then add to the must. Filter out any solids by pouring the mixture through a wire strainer lined with a couple of layers of cheesecloth. Since this must has very little solid material, you can put it directly into an airlocked fermentation vessel. The first fermentation will take about 3 weeks. Then rack the wine into bottles and allow it to ferment a second time (for 3 to 6 months) in the bottles. Put the corks into the bottles only about one-quarter of the way for the first month or two so carbon dioxide doesn't build up and burst the bottles. Then tap the corks firmly into place and cel- lar your wine. Wait at least 6 months before opening your first bottle.

SWEET APPLE WINE

This lovely dessert wine is sure to make you glad we don't have to do everything the way Great-grandpa did!

6 to 8 pounds ripe apples
1 pound light raisins
1 Campden tablet (optional)
1 teaspoon pectic enzyme
1 tablespoon citric acid *or* 2 ounces acid blend
1 package wine yeast (5–7 grams)
1 teaspoon yeast nutrient
1½ cups orange juice

Crush the apples in a fruit press and combine with the raisins in a 2-gallon plastic container. Add a Campden tablet, if desired, and let the mixture stand for 24 hours, well covered, stirring once or twice. Then strain out the solids and discard. Add the pectic enzyme, the acid, and enough water to make 1 gallon. Make a yeast starter-culture by combining the wine yeast and yeast nutrient with 1½ cups tepid orange juice. Cover, shake vigorously, and let stand until bubbly (1–3 hours); then add to the must. Filter the juice through cheesecloth and put it in an airlocked fermentation vessel. Ferment for 3 months initially; then rack the wine into bottles. Age in the bottles for an additional 6 to 12 months.

BLACKBERRY WINE

In those parts of the country where blackberries grow wild, finding their trailing canes along fence rows means luscious jellies and delicious wines are in the offing. But we've often wondered how a tablespoon of blackberry cordial got to be Great-grandfather's favorite cold remedy — in South Dakota, where blackberries don't grow. Grandma Idie assures us that it was even colder in South Dakota when she was a little girl than it is now, but her father always had some "blackberry remedy" on hand — perhaps he had it sent to him by relatives who lived in warmer climates.

At any rate, it must have been scarce. And that's probably why it was restricted to a single tablespoon at a time. Having tasted the results of these luscious blackberry country-wine recipes, we can see why Grandma still remembers her girlhood cold remedy with affection, even after more than eighty years!

    3½ pounds ripe blackberries
    1 Campden tablet (optional)
    1 teaspoon pectic enzyme
    1 package wine yeast (5–7 grams)
    1 teaspoon yeast nutrient
    1½ cups orange juice
    2¼ pounds sugar

Wash the berries carefully and then crush them in a 2-gallon sterilized plastic pail or wastebasket. Add a Campden tablet, if desired, and let stand for 24 hours, well covered. Then pour 2 quarts of boiling water over the mixture and let it cool. When completely cool, add the pectic enzyme. Make a yeast starter-culture by combining the wine yeast and yeast nutrient with 1 1/2 cups tepid orange juice. Cover, shake vigorously, and let stand until bubbly (1–3 hours); then add to the must. Cover the container with plastic wrap or aluminum foil and let it stand for 4 or 5 days. Then strain the mixture through cheesecloth and dissolve the sugar in the resulting juice. Add water to make 1 gallon. Pour the mixture into an airlocked fermentation vessel and let the wine clear. Rack the mixture into a sterilized jar and taste to see if it is sweet enough. If it isn't, stir in more sugar — up to 3/4 pound — and syphon the mixture into an airlocked vessel to complete fermentation. Rack the wine again and bottle it. Wait at least 6 months before opening your first bottle.

SWEET PORT-STYLE BLACKBERRY WINE

> 7 pounds blackberries
> 4 pounds sugar
> 1 Campden tablet (optional)
> 1/8 teaspoon tannin (if desired) or 1 tablespoon strong tea
> 1 package port-wine yeast (5–7 grams)
> 1 teaspoon yeast nutrient
> 1 1/2 cups white grape juice
> 1 orange

Crush all the berries a few at a time. Add the crushed berries, half the sugar, and 3 quarts of water to a 2-gallon plastic bucket or wastebasket. (You may add a Campden tablet to kill off any wild yeast that may be present on the fruit if you desire. If you do, let the mixture stand for 24 hours, well covered, before proceeding.) Then add the rest of the sugar, the tannin, and water to make 1 gallon. Make a yeast starter-culture by combining the wine yeast and yeast nutrient with the tepid grape juice. Cover, shake vigorously, and let stand until bubbly (1–3 hours); then add to the must. Ferment the mixture for 2 days and rack. Now add the juice and the grated rind (avoiding the white inner rind) of the orange. Ferment this mixture for 5 days. Rack the wine to clarify it, and let it sit for 5 more days. Rack into an airlocked fermentation vessel and allow the wine to ferment to completion. When you're sure that fermentation is complete, bottle, cork, and cellar the wine. Wait at least 6 months before opening your first bottle.

BLUEBERRY WINE

This recipe originally used wild blueberries, which gave an added piquancy to the wine. But today's winemaker can choose from a number of domesticated varieties that also result in a delicious blueberry wine. As with all wines, use whatever variety is most available and economical in your area.

> 1 gallon blueberries
> 1 teaspoon acid blend
> 1 Campden tablet (optional)
> 1 package wine yeast (5–7 grams)
> 1 teaspoon yeast nutrient
> 3 pounds sugar
> 1/4 teaspoon tannin

Crush the berries and set aside 1½ cups of the resulting juice for the yeast starter-culture. Put the crushed berries in a 2-gallon plastic bucket or wastebasket, add 2 quarts of boiling water and the acid blend (and 1 Campden tablet, if desired). Let the mixture stand for 24 hours, stirring two or three times in a pumping motion to introduce oxygen into the mixture. Make a yeast starter-culture by combining the wine yeast and yeast nutrient with the 1½ cups tepid blueberry juice. Cover, shake vigorously, and let stand until bubbly (1–3 hours); then add to the must. Boil half of the sugar in 1 quart of water and add to the must. Add the tannin and ferment for 2 days. Rack or strain and discard the solids. Then add the other half of the sugar and ferment for an additional 10 days. Add water to make a gallon if necessary. Rack the wine into an airlocked fermentation vessel and ferment to completion. Then bottle and cork the wine, and cellar it. You may sample at bottling time — nobody has that much willpower — but wait at least 6 months before you open the first bottle.

GOOSEBERRY WINE

Pluck a plump green gooseberry off the bush, pop it into your mouth, and be prepared to pucker up. With this pursed and pained expression on your face, people might think you're pondering some deep philosophical problem — and you are. You're wondering what perversity might inspire anyone to make wine from such an astringent and disagreeable little berry.

But Grandma knew that something magic happened to gooseberries when she added enough sugar and tucked them in between two slabs of flaky homemade pastry. And Grandpa, not to be outdone, found out that a little sugar and fermentation certainly improved the unadorned berry. You have to age gooseberry wine for at least a year, but we bet you'll think it was worth the wait.

> 5 pounds ripe, green gooseberries
> 1 teaspoon pectic enzyme
> 1 Campden tablet (optional)
> 1 package wine yeast (5–7 grams)
> 1 teaspoon yeast nutrient
> 1½ cups orange juice
> 2 pounds sugar

Remove the stem and the tail of the gooseberries and wash the fruit, making sure the berries are completely clean. Put them into a 2-gallon plastic bucket or wastebasket and squeeze them by hand until they are pulpy. Add pectic enzyme and enough water to make a gallon. Add the Campden tablet, if desired, and wait 24 hours. Make a yeast starter-culture by combining the wine yeast and yeast nutrient with 1½ cups tepid orange juice. Cover, shake vigorously, and let stand until bubbly (1–3 hours); then add to the must. Cover the container with plastic wrap or aluminum foil and let it stand for 3 days, stirring three or four times. Then strain out the solids and add the sugar. Put the mixture into an airlocked fermentation vessel and let it stand until it stops bubbling. Rack the wine and leave it to mature for about 6 months in an airlocked container. Rack into bottles and cork them, and cellar your wine. Gooseberry wine is best if you age it for at least a year after bottling.

Huckleberry Wine

Finding enough wild huckleberries to satisfy pie-making needs as well as winemaking ones must have been tough in the days before garden huckleberries became widely available. Fortunately, children of a bygone era seemed to regard wild-berry picking as a treat, so if a large family pooled their gleanings, they probably had enough berries for both endeavors. Huckleberries make a light, dry wine that complements fowl and seafood nicely.

>   1 gallon huckleberries
>   1 teaspoon acid blend *or* the juice of 3 citrus fruits
>   ¼ teaspoon tannin *or* 1 tablespoon strong tea, if desired
>   1 Campden tablet (optional)
>   1 package wine yeast (5–7 grams)
>   1 teaspoon yeast nutrient
>   1½ cups huckleberry juice
>   3 pounds sugar

Crush the berries in a 2-gallon plastic bucket or wastebasket and set aside 1½ cups of the resulting juice for the yeast starter-culture. Add 2 quarts of boiling water, the acid blend, and tannin or tea to the crushed berries. (You may add 1 Campden tablet at this time to kill any wild yeast that may be present.) Let the mixture stand for 24 hours, covered with foil or plastic wrap, stirring two or three times to introduce oxygen into the mixture. Make a yeast starter-culture by combining the wine yeast and yeast nutrient with the 1½ cups of huckleberry juice. Cover, shake vigorously, and let stand until bubbly (1–3 hours); then add to the must. Boil together half of the sugar and 1 quart of water. When it has cooled, add the sugar-water mixture to the must. Ferment for 5 days and rack or strain. Then add the rest of the sugar and ferment for 10 more days. Add water to make a gallon if necessary. Rack the wine into an airlocked fermentation vessel and allow it to ferment to completion. When fermentation stops, rack into bottles, cork, and cellar the wine. Wait at least 6 months before opening a bottle.

LOGANBERRY WINE

Boysenberries and loganberries are really large, wine-colored blackberry varieties. Although these varieties are available only in certain sections of the country, you can substitute any of the blackberry family members and get a perfectly delicious wine. Because we wanted to test every kind of wine in this book, we resorted to making a very small batch of loganberry wine from canned loganberries — certainly the expensive alternative. But then, we didn't have to do the picking and cleaning, so we enjoyed the ease with which we created this beautifully colored wine.

 2 1/2 pounds loganberries
 1 Campden tablet (optional)
 1 package wine yeast (5–7 grams)
 1 teaspoon yeast nutrient
 1 1/2 cups orange juice
 2 1/2 pounds sugar
 1/2 pint red grape-juice concentrate
 1 teaspoon acid blend *or* the juice of 3 citrus fruits

Begin your winemaking by pouring 2 quarts of boiling water over the berries in a 2-gallon plastic bucket or wastebasket. When the mixture has cooled, make it into a pulp with your hands and add a Campden tablet, if desired. Wait 24 hours. Make a yeast starter-culture by combining the wine yeast and yeast nutrient with 1 1/2 cups tepid orange juice. Cover, shake vigorously, and let stand until bubbly (1–3 hours); then add to the must. Let it stand for 4 days covered with foil or plastic wrap. Stir the mixture daily. Then strain it through cheesecloth and add the sugar and grape concentrate. Stir the mixture until the sugar is dissolved. Add the acid and enough water to make a gallon. Then put the mixture into an airlocked fermentation vessel and let it ferment to completion. When the wine is clear and no longer fermenting, rack it into bottles and cork and cellar the wine. Wait at least 6 months before opening a bottle.

Rose Hip Wine

Because roses and apples are different branches on the same family tree, you'll find that rose hip wine has a flavor reminiscent of apple wine, but more delicate. And like apples, rose hips need to be ripe before they taste sweet and mellow, so use only deep orange to red rose hips. Finally, make sure that you wash the rose hips thoroughly and be sure to know your source. Rose hips from bushes that have been treated with a systemic insecticide will contain traces of pesticide. For best flavor, gather rose hips from hedgerows in the fall after the first frost.

> 1½ pounds fresh rose hips *or* ½ pound dried rose hips
> 2¼ pounds sugar
> 1 Campden tablet (optional)
> 1 package wine yeast (5–7 grams)
> 1 teaspoon yeast nutrient
> 1½ cups orange juice
> 1 teaspoon citric acid *or* the juice of 1 lemon
> 1 teaspoon pectic enzyme

Wash the rose hips carefully and cut them in half. Then crush them in a 2-gallon plastic container. Add the sugar and pour 2 quarts of boiling water over the sugar and rose hips. Add a Campden tablet, if desired, and let sit, well covered, for 24 hours. Make a yeast starter-culture by combining the wine yeast and yeast nutrient with 1H cups tepid orange juice. Cover, shake vigorously, and let stand until bubbly (1–3 hours); then add to the must. Add the rest of the ingredients. Let the mixture stand for 1 week, stirring daily. Then strain out the solids and add enough water to make a gallon. Put into an airlocked fermentation vessel. Let the mixture stand for 3 months and then rack it. Let it ferment to completion, racking as often as necessary to ensure a fine, clear wine. (You'll be able to tell if your wine needs additional rackings if you notice a layer of sediment building up on the bottom of the container.) When the fermentation is complete, bottle, cork, and cellar the wine. Wait at least 2 to 3 months before you sample.

Raisin Wine

It's easy to forget that raisins are just dried grapes. That's why raisin wine is among the easiest of all wines to make. You could make raisin wine from little more than sugar, raisins, and water — and many country winemakers do. But, like undried grapes, raisins carry wild yeast on their skins, so making wine from just these three ingredients won't give you the same result every time. That's why we usually kill off the resident yeast and add wine yeast from a known source when we make wine from raisins.

> 1³/₄ pounds large raisins (dark or light)
> 1³/₄ pounds sugar
> 1 Campden tablet (optional)
> 1 teaspoon citric acid or acid blend
> 1 teaspoon pectic enzyme
> 1 package wine yeast (5–7 grams)
> 1 teaspoon yeast nutrient
> 1¹/₂ cups orange juice

Boil the raisins in 2 quarts of water for 1 minute in a large, unchipped, enamel or stainless steel pot. Let the mixture cool to room temperature and strain the liquor onto the sugar in a 2-gallon plastic bucket or wastebasket. Add a Campden tablet to kill the wild yeast if desired and let the mixture stand, well covered, for 24 hours. Then add the acid, the pectic enzyme, and water to make a gallon. Make a yeast starter-culture by combining the wine yeast and yeast nutrient with 1¹/₂ cups tepid orange juice. Cover, shake vigorously, and let stand until bubbly (1–3 hours); then add to the must. Pour the mixture into an airlocked fermentation vat. When the wine has cleared, rack and return to a clean airlocked fermentation vessel and ferment to completion. Then rack into bottles, cork, and cellar the wine. Wait at least 6 months before sampling.

Peach Wine

Use very ripe fruit, if available. Greener fruits have more pectin, so the wine is harder to clear. You may adjust your pectic enzyme according to how ripe the fruit is.

3–3½ pounds ripe peaches (about 10 peaches)
3 pounds sugar
1 teaspoon acid blend
½ teaspoon tannin *or* 1 tablespoon strong tea
1 Campden tablet (optional)
1 package wine yeast (5–7 grams)
1 teaspoon yeast nutrient
1½ cups orange juice
1–2 teaspoons pectic enzyme

Wash the peaches and slice them into a 2-gallon plastic wastebasket or bucket and toss in the pits. Add 2 quarts of boiled, cooled water in which you've dissolved half the sugar, acid blend, tannin or tea, and 1 Campden tablet if desired. (If you add a Campden tablet, wait 24 hours, stirring two or three times at intervals and keeping the container well covered, before proceeding.) Make a yeast starter-culture by combining the wine yeast and yeast nutrient with 1½ cups tepid orange juice. Cover, shake vigorously, and let stand until bubbly (1–3 hours); then add to the must. Add the pectic enzyme and ferment for 3 days. Rack or strain the wine into another wastebasket or bucket and discard the solids. Now boil the rest of the sugar in water to cover, let it cool, and add it to the other ingredients with enough water to make a gallon. Ferment for about 10 days or until the energetic bubbling slows down. Then rack the wine into a 1-gallon, airlocked fermentation vessel and ferment to completion. Bottle, cork, and cellar your wine. Wait at least 3 months before serving.

DRY RASPBERRY WINE

Delicate, fragile raspberries are the delight of the home garden, mostly because gardeners know that really good raspberries are few and far between in supermarkets. They don't ship well and even the most generous home growers don't really want to share. So most of us who don't grow our own settle for an occasional raspberry sundae or some raspberry jam on our toast. If you raise your own raspberries, raspberry wine is one way to save the essence of this delectable fruit (and maybe even share with those who are less wealthy).

2½ pounds raspberries
1 Campden tablet (optional)
2½ pounds sugar
½ pint red grape-juice concentrate
1 package wine yeast (5–7 grams)
1 teaspoon yeast nutrient
1½ cups orange juice
1 teaspoon pectic enzyme
1 teaspoon acid blend

Put the berries into a 2-gallon plastic bucket or wastebasket and pour 2 quarts of boiling water over them. When they have cooled to warm, make a pulp with your hands. Add the Campden tablet, if desired, and let the mixture sit for 4 days covered with plastic wrap or foil. Stir daily. At the end of 4 days, strain the mixture through cheesecloth and add the sugar and grape concentrate. Stir the liquid mixture until the sugar is dissolved. Make a yeast starter-culture by combining the wine yeast and yeast nutrient with 1½ cups tepid orange juice. Cover, shake vigorously, and let stand until bubbly (1–3 hours); then add to the must. Add the remaining ingredients and enough water to make a gallon and put the liquid into an airlocked fermentation vessel. When the fermentation is complete and the wine is clear, rack the wine into bottles and cork. You'll need to age this wine for at least 3 months for best flavor, and you'll never find the wait more difficult. Raspberry wines are so pretty and have such a delicious bouquet that waiting to sample them is the hardest part of the process.

SWEET RED RASPBERRY WINE

4 pounds ripe red raspberries
4 ounces light raisins
1 Campden tablet (optional)
1 package wine yeast (5–7 grams)
1 teaspoon yeast nutrient
1½ cups orange juice
4 pounds sugar
1 teaspoon acid blend

Be sure to use only ripe berries. Only a few green or partly green berries can change the flavor of the finished wine. Put the berries into a large, unchipped enamel or stainless steel container, crush, and add the raisins and 2 quarts of water. (Adding a Campden tablet at this point will kill any wild yeasts that are present. If you do this, let the mixture sit for 24 hours, well covered, before proceeding, stirring two or three times.) Make a yeast starter-culture by combining the wine yeast and yeast nutrient with 1 1/2 cups tepid orange juice. Cover, shake vigorously, and let stand until bubbly (1–3 hours); then add to the must. Strain the juice into a 2-gallon plastic bucket or wastebasket, discarding the pulp, and add half the sugar, the acid blend, and water to make 1 gallon. Allow the mixture to ferment for 5 days. Then rack and add the remaining sugar and ferment for 10 more days. Now rack the wine into an airlocked fermentation vessel and let it complete the fermentation process. When the wine is clear and no longer bubbling, rack into bottles, cork, and cellar the wine. Wait at least 6 months before opening a bottle.

WILD BLACK RASPBERRY WINE

This wine is all the more special because it's made from "found" bounty — those delectable black raspberries that grow along fence rows and ditches. Poison ivy seems to love the same locations, so beware when you harvest wild raspberries.

The delicate, dessert-quality flavor of black raspberry wine depends on the ripeness of the berries, and even a few green or partly green berries can change the flavor of the finished wine for the worse. Make sure your berries are completely ripe — even slightly overripe — for best results.

    4 pounds wild black raspberries
    8 ounces raisins
    1 teaspoon acid blend
    1 Campden tablet (optional)
    1 package wine yeast (5–7 grams)
    1 teaspoon yeast nutrient
    1 1/2 cups orange juice
    3 1/2 pounds sugar

Follow the instructions for Sweet Red Raspberry Wine on page 28.

Sweet Wild-Strawberry Dessert Wine

A fine finale to any meal! Lovely served with fresh fruit and cheese. If you can't find wild strawberries, cultivated strawberries will work, too.

    4 pounds wild strawberries
    4 ounces light raisins
    1 Campden tablet (optional)
    1 package wine yeast (5–7 grams)
    1 teaspoon yeast nutrient
    1 ½ cups orange juice
    1 teaspoon acid blend
    4 pounds sugar

Put washed and de-stemmed berries into a 2-gallon plastic bucket or wastebasket and crush. Add the raisins and 2 quarts water. (You may add 1 Campden tablet at this point to kill off any wild yeasts that are present on the berries. Let the mixture stand for 24 hours, well covered, stirring two to three times at intervals.) Strain through cheesecloth and discard the solids. Make a yeast starter-culture by combining the wine yeast and yeast nutrient with 1 ½ cups tepid orange juice. Cover, shake vigorously, and let stand until bubbly (1–3 hours); then add to the must. Add the acid blend and half of the sugar. Let the mixture ferment for 1 week. Add the rest of the sugar and enough water to make a gallon, and ferment the mixture for 10 days in an airlocked fermentation vessel. Rack into another airlocked vessel. Let the mixture ferment to completion and bottle, cork, and cellar the wine. Wait at least 6 months before opening a bottle.

Strawberry Wine

    3 pounds strawberries
    2 ½ pounds sugar
    1 Campden tablet (optional)
    1 package wine yeast (5–7 grams)
    1 teaspoon yeast nutrient
    1 ½ cups orange juice
    1 teaspoon citric acid *or* the juice of 1 lemon
    ½ teaspoon grape tannin *or* 1 tablespoon strong tea

Clean and de-stem the berries and put them into a 2-gallon plastic bucket or wastebasket. Then mash the sugar into the berries and add 2 quarts of water. Add the Campden tablet, if desired, and let the mixture stand for 24 hours, well covered, stirring two or three times at intervals. Pour the mixture into a large glass or plastic container and add water to make 1 gallon. Then strain out the solids and discard them. Make a yeast starter-culture by combining the wine yeast and yeast nutrient with 1½ cups tepid orange juice. Cover, shake vigorously, and let stand until bubbly (1–3 hours); then add to the must. Add the citric acid and tannin and put the mixture into a 1-gallon airlocked fermentation vessel. Allow the mixture to ferment to completion, racking as needed for clarity. When the wine has finished fermenting, bottle, cork, and cellar the wine. Wait at least 6 months before sampling.

ELDERBERRY WINE

This is a delicious, dark red wine that is prized as much for its beautiful color as it is for its full-bodied flavor. It may take a bit longer to complete the fermentation process than some other red wines, but when you serve it with rare roast beef, you'll agree that it was worth the wait!

   2½ pounds ripe elderberries
   1 Campden tablet (optional)
   1 package wine yeast (5–7 grams)
   1 teaspoon yeast nutrient
   1½ cups orange juice
   1 teaspoon acid blend *or* the juice of 2 lemons
   2½ pounds sugar

   Strip the berries from their stalks. (We use an ordinary table fork for stripping them. It's less messy and certainly less tedious than picking them off by hand.) Then weigh the berries without the stalks and crush them in a 2-gallon plastic wastebasket or bucket. Boil enough water to make a gallon in a large pan and pour it over the crushed berries. When the mixture has cooled, add the Campden tablet and wait 24 hours before proceeding. (If you don't use a Campden tablet, you may proceed as soon as the mixture has cooled.) Make a yeast starter-culture by combining the wine yeast and yeast nutrient with 1½ cups tepid orange juice. Cover, shake vigorously, and let stand until bubbly (1–3 hours); then add to the must. Add the acid blend. Let the mixture stand for 3 days, stirring daily. Then strain out the solids and add the sugar. At this point, transfer the wine to dark glass bottles so that the light doesn't affect the wine's color. We usually use two 1-gallon containers, filling each container only partially so that there's no bubbling over during the fermentation. (If you don't have dark glass 1-gallon containers, use clear glass ones and let the wine ferment in a dark closet.) You can stick a cotton ball or two into the necks of the bottles to keep out dust and fruit flies. When the fermentation slows, pour the two bottles together and affix an airlock, leaving about ³/₄ of an inch of space between the top of the wine and the bottom of the airlock. Then allow the wine to ferment to completion and bottle in dark green or brown bottles. Wait at least 6 months before you sample.

QUINCE WINE

This nice, dry wine has hints of pears and apples in its flavor. For those who've never seen a quince tree, the fruit is yellow to yellow-green and resembles a pear, although it doesn't have the classic pear shape. Instead, the fruit looks something like a fat donut, with depressions where the hole would be on either end.

> **20 ripe quinces**
> **2¹/₄ pounds sugar**
> **2 lemons**
> **1 teaspoon pectic enzyme**
> **1 Campden tablet (optional)**
> **1 package wine yeast (5–7 grams)**
> **1 teaspoon yeast nutrient**
> **1¹/₂ cups orange juice**

Grate the quinces as near to the core as possible and boil the grated pulp and peel over medium heat in water to cover for a maximum of 15 minutes in a large, unchipped enamel or stainless steel pot. (Don't overcook the fruit, or you may have trouble clearing the wine.) Strain the juice onto the sugar in a 2-gallon plastic bucket or wastebasket and add the juice and grated rind of the lemons (be careful to avoid the white inner rind). Let the mixture cool and add the pectic enzyme. Add a Campden tablet, if desired, and let the mixture sit for 24 hours, well covered. Make a yeast starter-culture by combining the wine yeast and yeast nutrient with 1½ cups tepid orange juice. Cover, shake vigorously, and let stand until bubbly (1–3 hours); then add to the must. Add water to make 1 gallon. Allow the mixture to ferment for 48 hours. Rack into an airlocked fermentation vessel and let the wine ferment to completion (about 9 months, racking at intervals as needed to clear the wine). When you are sure that fermentation is complete, bottle, cork, and cellar the wine. Age for at least 6 months before sampling.

MULBERRY WINE

Anyone who has a mulberry tree in the yard knows that mulberries can be a real pain in the neck. The fruit falls most of the summer, creating disagreeable purple stains on patios, shoes, and clothes. (They even cause birds to leave purple markers on your house and cars.) When you gather enough berries to make something of them, the stems are tough to remove and you end up with purple fingers and meager results. In fact, as far as we can tell, there's only one thing that mulberries are really good for, and that's making wine. Maybe that's why we found so many mulberry wine recipes.

We'd suggest that when you're ready to try your hand at mulberry wine, you spread a large piece of plastic or an old sheet on the ground under the tree and give the branches a good shaking. (We've always wanted to do that to mulberry trees, anyway.) It may take you several days to gather enough berries for a batch of wine, but the first ones will usually keep in the fridge and a few overripe berries won't hurt the wine. We don't even try to de-stem the mulberries as carefully as we'd have to for table use, since the solid materials will be strained out after a few days. Just wash the berries carefully, and you're ready to begin.

2½ pounds mulberries
½ pint red grape-juice concentrate
1½ pounds sugar
1 teaspoon pectic enzyme
1 Campden tablet (optional)
1 package wine yeast (5–7 grams)
1 teaspoon yeast nutrient
1½ cups orange juice

Put the cleaned berries into a 2-gallon plastic bucket or wastebasket and crush. Then add the grape concentrate and the sugar and cover with 2 quarts of boiling water. When the mixture has cooled, add the pectic enzyme (and a Campden tablet, if desired, to kill any wild yeasts that are present). Let the mixture sit for 24 hours, well covered. Make a yeast starter-culture by combining the wine yeast and yeast nutrient with 1½ cups tepid orange juice. Cover, shake vigorously, and let stand until bubbly (1–3 hours); then add to the must. Add enough water to make 1 gallon. Stir well and cover. Let the pulp ferment for 4 days and rack or strain, discarding the solids. Put the liquid in an airlocked fermentation vessel and when the wine has cleared and stopped bubbling, rack into bottles, cork, and cellar your wine. Wait at least 6 months before opening a bottle.

DRY MULBERRY WINE

> 3 pounds mulberries
> 1 pound gooseberries, crushed, or 1 pound green apples, chopped, or 1 pound light or dark raisins
> 1 orange
> 1 Campden tablet (optional)
> 1 teaspoon pectic enzyme
> 1 package wine yeast (5–7 grams)
> 1 teaspoon yeast nutrient
> 1½ cups orange juice
> 2–2½ pounds sugar

Wash and crush the mulberries in a 2-gallon plastic bucket or wastebasket. Add the crushed gooseberries, chopped apples, or raisins and the juice and grated rind (avoiding the white inner rind) of the orange to the must. Add a Campden tablet, if desired, and let sit, well covered, for 24 hours. Stir in the pectic enzyme and water to make 1 gallon. Make a yeast starter-culture by combining the wine yeast and yeast nutrient with 1½ cups tepid orange juice. Cover, shake vigorously, and let stand until bubbly (1–3 hours); then add to the must. Let the mixture sit for 5 to 7 days in a loosely covered container (foil or plastic wrap works fine). At the end of that time, strain the liquid into an airlocked fermentation vessel and ferment — without adding the sugar — for about 3 months. Then add 2 pounds sugar for a dry wine, or 2¹/₂ pounds for a semi-dry wine, and allow the wine to go through another fermentation. When the wine has cleared and the fermentation is complete, bottle the wine and age it for an additional 6 to 9 months.

SWEET MULBERRY WINE

5 pounds mulberries
1 teaspoon pectic enzyme
4 pounds sugar
1 Campden tablet (optional)
1 package wine yeast (5–7 grams)
1 teaspoon yeast nutrient
1¹/₂ cups orange juice
1 teaspoon acid blend
¹/₄ teaspoon tannin or 1 tablespoon strong tea, if desired

Crush the mulberries in a 2-gallon plastic bucket or wastebasket and pour 2 quarts of boiling water over them. Let the mixture cool. Then add the pectic enzyme and cover the container with plastic wrap or foil. Let it stand for 4 or 5 days, stirring daily. Strain the liquid through cheesecloth and add the sugar, stirring to dissolve. Add a Campden tablet, if desired, and let sit for 24 hours, well covered, before proceeding. Make a yeast starter-culture by combining the wine yeast and yeast nutrient with 1¹/₂ cups tepid orange juice. Cover, shake vigorously, and let stand until bubbly (1–3 hours); then add to the must. Add the remaining ingredients, plus enough water to make a gallon, and pour the liquid into an airlocked fermentation vessel. Let the wine complete the fermentation process, and when it is clear, rack and bottle the wine. Wait at least 6 months before opening your first bottle.

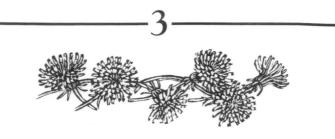

3

Wines from Flowers, Nuts, and More

When you serve wines made from the ingredients featured in this chapter, you'll be treating your guests to an experience they're unlikely to have at anyone else's table. Some of the old standards, like dandelion wine, offer delicious little sips of country-time nostalgia. Others, like the lovely, light almond wine on page 37, are enticing and exotic. You'll want to try making a few of these just for the surprise of them.

HAZELNUT WINE

> 1 ½ ounces hazelnuts
> 1 pound light raisins
> ½ pint white grape-juice concentrate
> 2 ¼ pounds sugar
> 2 lemons
> 1 Campden tablet (optional)
> 1 package wine yeast (5–7 grams)
> 1 teaspoon yeast nutrient
> 1 ½ cups orange juice
> 1 teaspoon pectic enzyme

First mince the hazelnuts and raisins — we use a food processor. Put the nuts and raisins in a large, unchipped enamel or stainless steel pot and add enough water to cover. Simmer gently for about an hour, making sure to keep enough water in the pan to prevent sticking. Strain the mixture into a 2-gallon plastic container and discard the solids. Add the concentrate and the sugar and enough water to make a gallon. Juice the 2 lemons and grate the outer rind, making sure you don't include the white inner rind. Add the lemon juice and the grated rind to the mixture. Add a Campden tablet, if desired, and let the mixture stand, well covered, for 24 hours. Make a yeast starter-culture by combining the wine yeast and yeast nutrient with 1 1/2 cups tepid orange juice. Cover, shake vigorously, and let stand until bubbly (1–3 hours); then add to the must. Add the pectic enzyme. Cover loosely and let the mixture ferment for about 10 days. Then rack it into an airlocked fermentation vessel and allow the wine to ferment to completion, racking as necessary to clear the wine. When you're sure the fermentation is complete, bottle, cork, and cellar the wine. Allow at least 3 additional months to pass before you sample.

ALMOND WINE

A little like a mild amaretto, almond wine is wonderful with desserts, especially pound cakes and cream-filled pastries. But it's equally good with fruit tarts — especially cherry, a fruit that complements the nutty wine to perfection.

1 1/2 ounces almonds
1 pound light raisins
1/2 pint white grape-juice concentrate
2 1/4 pounds sugar
2 lemons
1 Campden tablet (optional)
1 package wine yeast (5–7 grams)
1 teaspoon yeast nutrient
1 1/2 cups orange juice
1 teaspoon pectic enzyme

Mince the almonds and raisins — a food processor works well. Put the almonds and raisins in a large, unchipped enamel or stainless steel pot and add enough water to cover. Simmer the mixture gently for about an hour, making sure to keep enough water in the pan to prevent scorching. Strain the liquid into a 2-gallon plastic bucket or wastebasket and discard the solids. Add the grape-juice concentrate and enough water to make 1 gallon. Then add the sugar plus the juice of 2 lemons and their grated rind. (Make sure you don't include the white inner rind.) Add a Campden tablet, if desired, and let sit, well covered, for 24 hours. Make a yeast starter-culture by combining the wine yeast and yeast nutrient with 1½ cups tepid orange juice. Cover, shake vigorously, and let stand until bubbly (1–3 hours); then add to the must. Add the pectic enzyme and cover loosely. Allow the mixture to ferment for about 10 days. Then rack it to an airlocked fermentation vessel and let the wine ferment to completion, racking as necessary to clear the wine. Bottle, cork, and cellar the wine — and wait. This wine is best if you allow 3 months to pass before sampling.

CLOVE WINE

Clove wine may not be for everyone, but we like to make a batch or two about midsummer so it will be ready for the dozens of uses we find for it during the holiday season — starting with Halloween and continuing right up until the end of the year. It's a delightful addition to mulled wines and ciders and gives a distinctively different taste to eggnogs and sangrias. But our favorite use for clove wine is for soaking the cheesecloth coverings of our holiday fruitcakes — yum! And of course you can drink it — alone or as a refreshing addition to orange-garnished iced tea.

> 1 ounce whole cloves
> 2¼ pounds brown sugar
> 1 6-ounce can tangerine-juice concentrate
> 1 Campden tablet (optional)
> 1 package wine yeast (5–7 grams)
> 1 teaspoon yeast nutrient
> 1½ cups orange juice
> 1 teaspoon pectic enzyme

Tie the cloves into a coffee filter and simmer for about an hour in enough water to cover. Then put the sugar into a 2-gallon plastic container and add the liquor and 2 quarts of boiling water. Add the tangerine-juice concentrate. You may add the Campden tablet, if desired, and let the mixture stand, well covered, for 24 hours. Make a yeast starter-culture by combining the wine yeast and yeast nutrient with 1½ cups tepid orange juice. Cover, shake vigorously, and let stand until bubbly (1–3 hours); then add to the must. Add the pectic enzyme and enough water to make 1 gallon. Let the mixture stand for 4 days. Then place it in an airlocked fermentation vessel and let it sit until it clears. Rack several times at intervals until the wine remains clear, returning it each time to the airlocked vessel. When the fermentation is complete and the wine has cleared, bottle, cork, and cellar the wine. Wait at least 6 months before opening your first bottle.

CLOVE AND GINGER WINE

Wonderful wine coolers result from mixing this wine with lemon-lime soda or a tall glass of iced tea. But we like it best as a marinade for chicken that's to be seared in a wok or served sizzling from the grill. And if you like a little more spice to your fruitcakes, use clove and ginger wine for soaking.

    3 lemons
    1 orange
    1 ounce whole ginger root
    1 ounce whole cloves
    2¼ pounds light brown sugar
    1 Campden tablet (optional)
    1 package wine yeast (5–7 grams)
    1 teaspoon yeast nutrient
    1½ cups orange juice

Juice the lemons and the orange and set the juice aside. Grate the rind from the lemons and the orange (avoiding the white inner rind) and place the grated rind in a small muslin bag. Bruise the ginger and add it and the cloves to the bag. (Or use a coffee filter to hold these ingredients and tie it shut with several windings of strong thread.) Place the bag in 2 quarts of boiling water and simmer in a non-aluminum saucepan for 1 hour. Then put the sugar into a 2-gallon plastic container and pour the boiling water over it. Add the citrus juice. Add the Campden tablet, if desired, and let the mixture stand, well covered, for 24 hours. Make a yeast starter-culture by combining the wine yeast and yeast nutrient with 1½ cups tepid orange juice. Cover, shake vigorously, and let stand until bubbly (1–3 hours); then add to the must. Add water to make a gallon, and cover the container loosely. Let it stand for 4 days. Then rack the mixture into an airlocked fermentation vessel and let it ferment, racking as necessary to clear the wine. When the fermentation is complete, bottle, cork, and cellar the wine. This one's a good keeper. Wait at least 6 months before sampling.

CORNMEAL WINE

Cornmeal wine is a bit slower initially than many other wines, so be patient with it. Once it gets going, it makes a good, dry wine.

3 oranges
2 lemons
1 1/2 pounds cornmeal
2 1/4 pounds sugar
3 pints white grape-juice concentrate
1 tablespoon ground uncooked rice (use a food processor or blender)
1 Campden tablet (optional)
1 package wine yeast (5–7 grams)
1 teaspoon yeast nutrient
1 1/2 cups orange juice

Squeeze the juice from the oranges and lemons and grate the outer rind. (Discard the solids and the white inner rind.) Mix the first six ingredients in a 2-gallon plastic container. Add enough water to make a gallon. Add a Campden tablet, if you choose, and let the mixture sit, well covered, for 24 hours. Make a yeast starter-culture by combining the wine yeast and yeast nutrient with 1 1/2 cups tepid orange juice. Cover, shake vigorously, and let stand until bubbly (1–3 hours); then add to the must. Let the mixture sit for 30 days, loosely covered. Strain out the solids and transfer the liquid to a 1-gallon airlocked fermentation vessel and let it ferment for 30 days more. When fermentation is complete, bottle the wine, cork it, and store in a cool cellar. Wait 6 months or more before opening a bottle.

DANDELION WINE

Country folks had an optimistic and ecologically sound solution to dande-
lion problems — they made dandelion wine. Once you've tried a little of this
golden nectar, you'll know why Ray Bradbury called it "bottled sunshine."

The key to making delicious dandelion wine is being careful to use clean,
chemical-free petals — and only petals. The green stuff that surrounds the
dandelion flower will give your wine an off taste, so be sure to peel it back
and then pull or cut the petals from the stem. Dandelion wine has such a
delicate flavor, we prefer to use acid blend rather than citrus to avoid too
much citrus taste, but if you're careful not to get the inner rind into the
mixture, citrus works well enough.

> 6 cups dandelion petals
> 2 pounds sugar
> 1 pound light raisins
> 3 teaspoons acid blend *or* the juice of 2 lemons and 1
>   orange
> 1 Campden tablet (optional)
> 1 package wine yeast (5–7 grams)
> 1 teaspoon yeast nutrient
> 1 1/2 cups orange juice

Wash and prepare the dandelion petals. Place the first four ingredients in a 2-gallon plastic wastebasket or pail. Bring a gallon of water
to a boil and pour it over them. (If you'd like to add a Campden tablet
to kill off wild yeasts, now is the time. If you use one, let the mixture
sit for 24 hours, well covered, before proceeding.) Cool the mixture
to lukewarm. Make a yeast starter-culture by combining the wine
yeast and yeast nutrient with 1 1/2 cups tepid orange juice. Cover, shake
vigorously, and let stand until bubbly (1–3 hours); then add to the
must. Ferment for 3 days in the original container, loosely covered
with plastic wrap or a sheet of foil. Then rack the liquid into a 1-gallon
airlocked fermentation vessel and allow it to ferment to completion
— about 3 months. Rack again. When you're sure the fermentation
is complete, bottle, cork, and cellar the wine. Wait at least 6 months
before sampling the wine.

3 ounces whole ginger root
$1/2$ pint white grape-juice concentrate
$1 1/2$ pounds bananas
1 Campden tablet (optional)
1 package wine yeast (5–7 grams)
1 teaspoon yeast nutrient
$1 1/2$ cups orange juice
2 pounds sugar
1 teaspoon pectic enzyme

Start by cutting up the ginger root into pieces and adding it to the grape concentrate in a 2-gallon plastic container. Add 2 quarts of boiling water. Peel the bananas and force them through a strainer; add to the ginger mixture. Add a Campden tablet, if desired, and let sit, well covered, for 24 hours. Make a yeast starter-culture by combining the wine yeast and yeast nutrient with $1 1/2$ cups tepid orange juice. Cover, shake vigorously, and let stand until bubbly (1–3 hours); then add to the must. Add the remaining ingredients and water to make a gallon. Let the pulp ferment, loosely covered, for 10 days. Then rack into an airlocked fermentation vessel and let the mixture ferment for at least 3 months, racking as necessary to clear the wine. When fermentation is complete, bottle, cork, and cellar the wine. Wait 6 months or more before opening a bottle.

ELDERFLOWER WINE I

If you just can't wait for the elderberries, try elderflowers instead!

1 lemon
1 pint elderflower heads (tightly packed)
1 Campden tablet (optional)
3 pounds sugar
1 teaspoon pectic enzyme
1 package wine yeast (5–7 grams)
1 teaspoon yeast nutrient
$1 1/2$ cups orange juice

Grate the lemon rind (avoiding the white inner rind) and add it to a 2-gallon, sterilized plastic container with the elderflowers (be sure to wash them thoroughly, especially if they grew near a road). Reserve the lemon. Bring a gallon of water to a boil and pour it over the rind-elderflower mixture. Add a Campden tablet, if desired. Let the mixture sit for 3 days, well covered. Then pour the mixture over the sugar in a large stainless steel or unchipped enamel container and bring it to a boil. When it has cooled to lukewarm, strain it into an airlocked fermentation vessel and add the pectic enzyme and the juice from the lemon. Make a yeast starter-culture by combining the wine yeast and yeast nutrient with 1 1/2 cups tepid orange juice. Cover, shake vigorously, and let stand until bubbly (1–3 hours); then add to the must. Let the fermentation proceed to completion, racking as necessary to clear the wine. The time from start to bottling is usually about 4 months. Wait at least 6 months before opening your first bottle.

ELDERFLOWER WINE II

3/4 pint (3 ounces) fresh elderflowers *or* H ounce dried
   flowers
3 lemons
1/2 pound light raisins *or* 1/4 pint white grape-juice
   concentrate
1 Campden tablet (optional)
2 3/4 pounds sugar
1 teaspoon tannin
1 package wine yeast (5–7 grams)
1 teaspoon yeast nutrient
1 1/2 cups orange juice

Cut the washed elderflowers from their stems with scissors and grate the lemon rinds (avoiding the white inner rind). Reserve the lemons. Mix the grated rind with the elderflowers in a large unchipped enamel or stainless steel pot and pour 2 quarts of boiling water over them. Cool. Add the raisins and a Campden tablet, if desired, and let sit for 3 days, loosely covered with plastic wrap or foil. Add the sugar and bring the mixture to a boil. Continue to simmer for 5–6 minutes. Let the mixture cool and strain it into a 2-gallon plastic container.

Juice the lemons and add the lemon juice and the tannin. Make a yeast starter-culture by combining the wine yeast and yeast nutrient with 1½ cups tepid orange juice. Cover, shake vigorously, and let stand until bubbly (1–3 hours); then add to the must. Add water to make a gallon. Let stand until clear. Then rack the mixture into an airlocked fermentation vessel and let stand for about 2 months. Rack again and bottle when the fermentation is complete. Wait at least 6 months before sampling.

HONEYSUCKLE WINE

Honeysuckle wine captures an elusive essence of spring that's almost — but not quite — subliminal. It's soft and subtle alone and delectable in summer wine coolers. Do not, however, make wine from honeysuckle berries. They're poisonous.

> 2 pints honeysuckle blossoms (pressed down lightly)
> 2¼ pounds sugar
> 4 ounces white grape-juice concentrate
> 2 teaspoons citric acid *or* the juice of 3 citrus fruits
> 1 Campden tablet (optional)
> 1 package wine yeast (5–7 grams)
> 1 teaspoon yeast nutrient
> 1½ cups orange juice
> 1 teaspoon tannin *or* 1 tablespoon strong tea

Wash the honeysuckle blossoms using a colander and cold water. Then place the flowers, half the sugar, the grape concentrate, and the citric acid or citrus juice in a 2-gallon plastic container and add enough water to make a gallon. (Add a Campden tablet if desired and let the mixture sit, well covered, for 24 hours.) Make a yeast starter-culture by combining the wine yeast and yeast nutrient with 1½ cups tepid orange juice. Cover, shake vigorously, and let stand until bubbly (1–3 hours); then add to the must. Add the tannin and allow the mixture to ferment, loosely covered, for 7 days. Rack the liquid into a 1-gallon airlocked fermentation vessel and let it ferment to completion, racking as necessary to clear the wine. When the fermentation is complete, bottle, cork, and cellar the wine. Wait 6 months or more before sampling.

Rose Petal Wine

We like to use red roses to make this wine so that the resulting liquid is pink and perfect — as delicate to look at as it is to drink.

Again, a word of caution about rose wines. Make sure that the rose petals you use come from bushes that haven't been treated with a systemic insecticide, and wash the petals carefully before you use them.

    2 quarts rose petals
    2 pounds sugar
    1/2 pint white grape-juice concentrate
    1 Campden tablet (optional)
    1 teaspoon citric acid
    1 package wine yeast (5–7 grams)
    1 teaspoon yeast nutrient
    1 1/2 cups orange juice

Bring a gallon of water to a boil in a large saucepan. Add rose petals, sugar, and grape concentrate. Remove from the heat and cool. Add a Campden tablet, if desired, and let sit, well covered, for 24 hours. Add the citric acid. Make a yeast starter-culture by combining the wine yeast and yeast nutrient with 1 1/2 cups tepid orange juice. Cover, shake vigorously, and let stand until bubbly (1–3 hours); then add to the must. Place the mixture in a 2-gallon plastic bucket or wastebasket, cover loosely, and let sit for 1 week. Then rack the liquid into a 1-gallon airlocked fermentation vessel. Rack as needed to clear the wine, and, when fermentation has stopped, rack the wine into bottles, cork, and cellar. Wait 6 months before opening a bottle.

White Clover Wine

    1 gallon white clover heads
    3 pounds sugar
    1 Campden tablet (optional)
    1 package wine yeast (5–7 grams)
    1 teaspoon yeast nutrient
    1 1/2 cups orange juice
    Juice of 2 lemons

Pull the petals from the clover heads and discard the base of the flowers. Put the petals in a large stainless steel or enamel pot with about 3½ quarts of water and bring the mixture to a boil. Remove the pan from the heat and add half of the sugar. Add a Campden tablet, if desired, and let sit, well covered, for 24 hours. Make a yeast starter-culture by combining the wine yeast and yeast nutrient with 1½ cups tepid orange juice. Cover, shake vigorously, and let stand until bubbly (1–3 hours); then add to the must. Add lemon juice. Transfer to a 2-gallon plastic container and ferment for 5 days, loosely covered. Then add the rest of the sugar and stir until it's dissolved. Rack and ferment the juices for 10 more days. Then rack into a 1-gallon airlocked fermentation vessel and let the wine ferment to completion. When fermentation is finished, bottle, cork, and cellar the wine. Wait 6 months before sampling.

RED CLOVER WINE

    1 gallon red clover heads
    3 pounds sugar
    8 ounces light raisins
    1 Campden tablet (optional)
    1 teaspoon acid blend *or the juice and rind of 3 citrus fruits*
    1 package wine yeast (5–7 grams)
    1 teaspoon yeast nutrient
    1½ cups orange juice

De-stem the clover heads and discard the base of the flowers. Place the petals in a large enamel or stainless steel saucepan with a gallon of water and bring the mixture to a boil. Remove from the heat and add half the sugar and the raisins. Cool. Add a Campden tablet, if desired, and let sit, well covered, for 24 hours. Then transfer to a 2-gallon plastic container and add the acid blend. Make a yeast starter-culture by combining the wine yeast and yeast nutrient with 1½ cups tepid orange juice. Cover, shake vigorously, and let stand until bubbly (1–3 hours); then add to the must. Allow the mixture to sit for 5 days, loosely covered. Add the rest of the sugar, re-cover, and wait another 7 days. Then rack into an airlocked fermentation vessel and wait another 5 days. If the fermentation is complete at this time and the wine has cleared, you may bottle and loosely cork the wine. If you don't get any cork-popping within several days, force the corks completely into the bottles and cellar the wine. Wait 6 months or more before sampling.

MARIGOLD WINE

> 1 lemon
> 2 oranges
> 2½ to 3½ quarts marigold flower petals (without sepals and stems)
> 3 pounds sugar
> 1 Campden tablet (optional)
> 1 package wine yeast (5–7 grams)
> 1 teaspoon yeast nutrient
> 1½ cups orange juice

Grate the rind of the lemon and oranges (avoiding the white inner rind) and place the grated rind in a 2-gallon plastic container with the flower petals. Reserve the fruit. Bring a gallon of water to a boil, pour over the flower-petal mixture, and add the sugar, stirring until it is dissolved. Cool. Add the Campden tablet, if desired, and let sit, well covered, for 24 hours. Make a yeast starter-culture by combining the wine yeast and yeast nutrient with 1½ cups tepid orange juice. Cover, shake vigorously, and let stand until bubbly (1–3 hours); then add to the must. Juice the lemon and oranges and add the juice. Let the mixture sit for 7 days, loosely covered. Then strain out the solids and transfer the liquid to a 1-gallon airlocked fermentation vessel. Allow the wine to ferment to completion — usually 3 to 4 weeks. Then rack the wine and, if fermentation is complete, bottle, cork, and cellar the wine. Wait at least 6 months before sampling the wine.

POTATO WINE

In Kentucky and Tennessee, old-timers often tell of adding potatoes to their wine recipes to increase the alcohol content and the keeping qualities. This recipe makes a white wine that can be used in much the same way as vodka for a not-quite Virgin Mary or a simply smashing Screwdriver. But because naturally fermented beverages don't have more than 18 percent alcohol, adding wine in the same proportion as you'd add vodka when you make these drinks results in a lighter, less alcoholic beverage.

    3 pounds old potatoes
    4 pounds sugar
    4 ounces chopped light raisins
    2 lemons
    2 oranges
    1 Campden tablet (optional)
    1 package wine yeast (5–7 grams)
    1 teaspoon yeast nutrient
    1 1/2 cups orange juice

Scrub the potatoes but don't peel them. Cut them into quarters and cut away any bad spots or hollow centers. Then grate them into a large, unchipped enamel or stainless steel pot and add 3 quarts of water. Bring to a boil and simmer for about 15 minutes, removing any scum that comes to the top. Continue to simmer until scum ceases rising. Put the sugar and the chopped raisins into a 2-gallon plastic container and strain the potato water onto them. Juice the lemons and oranges and grate the outer rind (avoiding the white inner rind). Add the grated rind and juice of the lemons and oranges. Cool. Add a Campden tablet, if desired, and let sit, well covered, for 24 hours. Make a yeast starter-culture by combining the wine yeast and yeast nutrient with 1 1/2 cups orange juice. Cover, shake vigorously, and let stand until bubbly (1–3 hours); then add to the must. Add water to make a gallon if needed. Let the mixture sit for 7 days, loosely covered. Rack and let the mixture sit for 10 more days in a same-size container. Rack again, this time into a 1-gallon airlocked fermentation vessel. Allow the wine to ferment to completion and bottle, cork, and cellar the wine. Wait 6 months or more before opening your first bottle.

³/₄ pound wheat berries
1 pound light raisins *or* 1 pint white grape-juice concentrate
2¹/₂ pounds brown sugar
1 Campden tablet (optional)
1 package wine yeast (5–7 grams)
1 teaspoon yeast nutrient
1¹/₂ cups orange juice
1 ounce citric acid
1 teaspoon pectic enzyme

Soak the wheat berries overnight in 1 pint of water to soften them. Mince the wheat berries and raisins (a food processor works well) and put them in a 2-gallon plastic container. Bring 2 quarts of water to a boil, pour it over the wheat-raisin mixture, and add the sugar. Cool. Add a Campden tablet, if desired, and let sit, well covered, for 24 hours. Make a yeast starter-culture by combining the wine yeast and yeast nutrient with 1¹/₂ cups orange juice. Cover, shake vigorously, and let stand until bubbly (1–3 hours); then add to the must. Add the citric acid and the pectic enzyme and let the mixture sit, loosely covered, for 10 days, stirring daily. Add water to make a gallon if needed. Then rack the mixture into a 1-gallon airlocked fermentation vessel and allow it to ferment to completion. When fermentation stops, bottle, cork, and cellar the wine. Wait 6 months or more before opening a bottle.

4

Meads, Melomels, and Metheglins

*H*ave you ever noticed how many heroines of romantic fiction have "kisses sweeter than wine"? Lips that "taste like honey"?

Both wine and honey spark the imagination with images of things delicious and desirable. If you've never understood just why that is so, then you probably haven't been lucky enough to sample meads, melomels, or metheglins, the three kinds of honey wines that you can create in nearly infinite numbers of combinations.

Honey wines are usually full bodied and delicious — enjoyable with poultry main dishes, with desserts, or as creative additions to your favorite recipes calling for wine. And they are not difficult to make once you understand the special requirements of honey-based wines.

By itself, honey makes a pretty unsatisfactory wine. Although honey provides the energy the wine yeast needs to live, it's deficient in some of the essential organic nutrients necessary for sustained growth. If you don't provide these nutrients, the fermentation process proceeds for a short time — until whatever nutrients that are there are used up — and then the process stops. You'll end up with a sticky-sweet, low-alcohol concoction that only gets worse with age.

To make good honey wines, you need to provide nutrients for the yeast to continue its growth. You can do this in one of two ways — by using a commercial yeast nutrient or by adding fruits or juices to your recipe. Adding a commercial yeast nutrient is a simple, efficient way to make sure your wine completes the fermentation process. You can buy it anywhere you find other wine-making supplies. If you prefer the totally natural approach, you can add fruits to provide the nutrients and get a flavor bonus, too.

Melomels usually don't need additional nutrients, because their ingredients include fruit by definition, but commercial yeast nutrients do speed up a melomel's fermentation. Meads and metheglins do need additional nutrients, and those nutrients can be added in the form of fruit or fruit juice, which would seem to blur the distinctions among these wines. The differences are in the primary flavor, however. Meads taste of honey — even if some fruit has been added; melomels taste of the fruit-and-honey combination; and metheglins, delightfully different honey wines, taste — well, like romance itself.

Honey wines also need an acid component to give them a necessary tartness; most winemakers add either a commercial acid blend or citrus juice. Even with some recipes that call for fruits, you may want to add an acid blend to achieve the desirable acidity. Adding a little acid almost always improves the flavor of the wine, imparting a pleasant tang to the taste.

The flavor of the honey doesn't seem to make much difference in the wines, so we haven't usually specified the flavor of honey to use in a particular recipe. We suggest that you experiment, starting with what you like best.

As you look at the recipes for these different kinds of honey wines, you'll see that the distinctions seem pretty academic. For convenience, we treat the different kinds of honey wines as though the categories were separate and distinct. But we bet it never occurred to early country winemakers to worry about such distinctions. Like Dom Perignon, whose real claim to fame — champagne fanciers might disagree — was that he blended country wines to achieve the flavors he wanted, they were interested in good-tasting wines. Dom Perignon became the romantic figure of champagne fame because he experimented until he found the perfect combinations of flavors to suit his taste. In the process, he showed champagne makers how to achieve consistently fine wines.

MAKING MEADS

Made correctly, mead has good body and great flavor. The only way to produce mead flavored *only* by honey is to add yeast nutrient and acid to the honey, water, and yeast mixture. You can also make a delicious mead by using fruit juice as a substitute for the acid blend and allowing the rich honey taste to dominate. Why not try both methods to see which you like best? Either produces a fine mead.

If you decide to buy winemaking ingredients from commercial sources, you'll need three major ingredients: yeast, yeast nutrient, and acid blend. The yeast nutrient contains ammonium compounds, trace elements, and vitamins. Acid blend (or citric acid) provides the acid component that's necessary for good wine flavor and helps create the right environment for yeast growth. It also has a slight preservative action.

Since commercial yeast nutrients vary somewhat according to the source, use the amount of yeast nutrient recommended by the supplier. You can vary the amount of acid you add according to your taste once you have some experience. Until then, start with 1 ounce of acid blend per gallon of wine. (Later you may want to vary it from ½ ounce to 1½ ounces per gallon.) Whatever amount you use, be sure to write down the blend so you can duplicate it, just in case you've made the perfect mead.

Be sure to write down the amount of fruit additives, too. Your wine will still be a mead as long as the taste of honey is preserved or enhanced by the added fruit.

The simplest way to make a natural mead is to add one 6-ounce can of frozen citrus-juice concentrate per gallon of honey wine. The concentrate provides both nutrients and acidity, but it will affect the taste, too. Since most commercial citrus juices are made from the whole fruit, which contains some of the bitter inner rind, you could pick up some unwanted bitterness using this method. A better way is to fresh-squeeze the juice yourself and add the finely grated outer rind for flavor, being careful not to include any of the bitter white inner rind.

Nutrients can also come from grain (such as wheat), other fruits (such as grapes), or vegetables (such as potatoes). Any of these let the yeast grow properly. When you pick a natural yeast nutrient, be aware that fruits have an acid component whereas vegetables and grains do not. If your nutrient source is low-acid (see page 132), then the juice of a couple of lemons or oranges or some acid blend will give your wine some tartness.

Finally, if you're concerned about the appearance of your wine, you can add some pectic enzyme to the mixture. Pectic enzyme digests the pectin in fruits and the waxy substances in honey, which frequently cause cloudy wines.

Some experts suggest that you age meads from 5 to 7 years! But we've never been patient enough to wait that long. You may want to make enough mead to track its development over a period of years by tasting some every 6 months. We do have one special mead in our cellar that we plan to open on New Year's Eve at the turn of the century.

For those of you who are eager to get started, here are some recipes we've used successfully.

MEAD

> 3 pounds honey
> 1 tablespoon citric acid *or* 2 tablespoons acid blend
> 1 teaspoon pectic enzyme
> 1 Campden tablet (optional)
> 1 package champagne yeast (5–7 grams)
> 1 teaspoon yeast nutrient
> 1 1/2 cups orange juice

Boil the honey in water (1 part honey to 2 parts water — use the empty honey jar to measure the water) in a large enamel or stainless steel pot for 10 to 20 minutes, skimming off any foam that forms. (The foam will contain any impurities in the water and the small amount of beeswax that remains in the honey when it's processed.) Let the mixture cool and transfer the honey-water mixture to a 2-gallon plastic container. Add the acid, the pectic enzyme, and water to make a gallon. Add the Campden tablet and let the mixture sit, well covered, for 24 hours. Make a yeast starter-culture by combining the champagne yeast and yeast nutrient with 1½ cups tepid orange juice. Cover, shake vigorously, and let stand until bubbly (1–3 hours); then add to the must. Allow the mixture to ferment. We recommend racking meads after the most vigorous fermentation. At this time, syphon the wine into a 1-gallon airlocked fermentation vessel. Rack into another airlocked container in about 3 months and once again in about 6 months. Rack again right before bottling — about a year after fermentation started. Then bottle and cork the finished mead and store it in a cool cellar for 6 months or more before opening a bottle.

NATURAL MEAD

> 3 pounds orange blossom honey
> 1 6-ounce can tangerine-juice concentrate *or* 1 pint juice
>   and 1 tablespoon grated rind of a fresh tangerine
> 1 teaspoon pectic enzyme
> 1 Campden tablet (optional)
> 1 package champagne yeast (5–7 grams)
> 1 teaspoon yeast nutrient
> 1½ cups orange juice
> 1 sweet orange (optional)

Begin by boiling a honey-water mixture (1 part honey to 2 parts water — use the empty honey jar to measure the water) in a large enamel or stainless steel pot and skimming off the foam to remove impurities. When the mixture has cooled to lukewarm, transfer it to a 2-gallon plastic container and add the concentrate or fruit juice, the pectic enzyme, and water to make a gallon. Add the Campden tablet and cover the mixture for 24 hours before proceeding. Make a yeast starter-culture by combining the champagne yeast and yeast nutrient with 1½ cups tepid orange juice. Cover, shake vigorously, and let stand until bubbly (1–3 hours); then add to the must. You may add some thinly grated rind from a sweet orange for some additional subtle flavoring, but use a vegetable peeler to remove it so you don't get any of the white inner rind; it will make your wine bitter.

Allow the mixture to ferment, loosely covered, until the bubbling slows down. Then rack the wine into a 1-gallon airlocked container and let it ferment for about 3 months. Rack into another container that can be fitted with an airlock, and rack every 3 months until the wine is clear and sparkling. Then rack into bottles, putting the corks only one-fourth of the way into the bottles until you are sure that fermentation is complete. Tap the corks into place and cellar the wine. Wait at least a year before drinking.

SWEET DESSERT MEAD

This is a golden nectar to serve with the most luscious dessert — a fitting finish to any elegant meal. You may fortify this wine by adding 1 to 2 cups of Grand Marnier or brandy to improve aging and keeping qualities; age for an additional 6 months if you do.

> 4 pounds honey
> 1 tablespoon acid blend
> 2 teaspoons pectic enzyme
> Thinly grated rind (outer rind only) of 1 sweet orange
> 1 Campden tablet (optional)
> 1 package champagne yeast (5–7 grams)
> 1 teaspoon yeast nutrient
> 1 1/2 cups orange juice

Follow the directions for making mead on page 53, adding the orange rind at the same time you add the acid blend and pectic enzyme.

MAKING MELOMELS

Some of the best country wines we've ever tried are melomels. The combination of honey and fruit produces fruity, tangy wines with lovely bouquets and sound body. The different flavors are limited only by the fruits that are available. Melomels are perfect for home gardeners who have a choice of fruits harvested from their own backyard berry patch or home orchard. The marriage of fruit and honey to make wine solves the yeast-nutrient problem that occurs when making wines with only honey. If the fruit used to make wine is low in acid, the juice of three citrus fruits — one lemon and two oranges, for example — will provide the necessary acid for a gallon of wine. If you are a beginning winemaker, we strongly suggest that you try at least one melomel. Once you do, a whole new world of fine wines becomes available to you — and they're easy, so you're almost certain to succeed.

The general method we use to develop melomel recipes is to start with 3 pounds of honey, 1–3 pounds of fresh fruit, and citrus juice, if required. Melomels may be as difficult to clear as meads because of waxy impurities in the honey, so we generally boil the honey in two times its volume of water for 10 to 20 minutes and skim off the foam that rises to the surface. (You can use the empty honey jar to measure the water.) Cloudy wine is not harmful to drink, but the clear, sparkling color of properly cleared wine, served in crystal-clear glasses, is part of a wine's charm.

After you've finished this first step, add the fruit to the still-hot mixture and allow it to sit for 24 hours. The waiting period lets the full fruit flavor permeate the mixture. Then strain the liquid into a jug that can be fitted with a fermentation lock. Allowing some of the smaller fruit fragments to enter the jug provides nutrients for yeast growth.

Add pectic enzyme and yeast starter-culture (see page 15 for more information on yeast starter-cultures). We like to use champagne yeast for most of our melomels; it gives honey wines a delicious flavor and produces a nice firm sediment for easier racking — an important consideration, since honey wines are sometimes hard to clear. Then allow fermentation to begin. After 3 months, rack the wine, but wait at least 6 months before bottling it. If bubbles are present after moving the wine to a warm room for 24 hours, your wine isn't ready for bottling. Try again in a month. If the fermentation still isn't complete, wait another month. If a longer waiting period is necessary, be sure to rack the wine at least every 3 months until it's bottled. With each racking, the wine becomes clearer and more beautiful. Your guests will love these wines, so be sure to make an extra batch for creative gift-giving.

We've made all of the following melomels; each is a favorite. When we looked for old country-wine recipes, collecting family favorites from amateur winemakers and creating some of our own, we made dozens of melomels. Our "panel of experts" — friends and family members who were more than willing to attend an occasional wine-tasting — chose these as best. But don't be limited by these recipes. Experiment. Creating richly flavored melomels to your own taste and resources is part of the fun of winemaking.

CHERRY MELOMEL

This wine is semi-sweet with an especially delightful bouquet — and the taste is superb. You may fortify this wine — kirsch or cherry brandy works well. For an exceptionally sweet dessert wine, add a little more honey.

> 3 pounds clover honey
> 1 pound cherries (dark or sour)
> 1 tablespoon acid blend *or* the juice of 1 lemon and 2 oranges
> 1 Campden tablet (optional)
> 1 package champagne yeast (5–7 grams)
> 1 teaspoon yeast nutrient
> 1 1/2 cups orange juice

Boil the honey with water (2 parts water to 1 part honey) in a large enamel or stainless steel pot and skim the resulting foam from the top of the mixture. Separately, in a non-aluminum saucepan, boil the cherries in a small amount of water. Allow the honey-water mixture and the cherries to cool. Then put the honey mixture, the juice from the cherries, the acid blend (or citrus juices), and water to make 1 gallon into a 2-gallon plastic container. Add the Campden tablet, if desired, and let the mixture sit, well covered, for 24 hours. Make a yeast starter-culture by combining the champagne yeast and yeast nutrient with 1H cups tepid orange juice. Cover, shake vigorously, and let stand until bubbly (1–3 hours); then add to the must. Cover the container loosely.

After 10 days, rack into a 1-gallon airlocked fermentation vessel and ferment the wine for 3 months; then rack again. Bottle after 6 more months if fermentation is complete and wait another 6 months before opening.

Raspberry Melomel

Raspberry melomel has an intense raspberry flavor — a little like sipping the essence of raspberries fresh from the garden. We particularly enjoy this wine in winter, when the snow is piled outside and summer's fresh raspberries are only a dream.

>   3 pounds orange blossom honey
>   2 pounds raspberries
>   1 Campden tablet (optional)
>   1 package champagne yeast (5–7 grams)
>   1 teaspoon yeast nutrient
>   1 1/2 cups orange juice
>   1 tablespoon acid blend *or* the juice of 1 lemon and 2
>   oranges

Remove impurities from the honey by boiling with 2 parts water in a large enamel or stainless steel pot and skimming off the foam. Cool. Crush berries and add to a 2-gallon plastic container with the honey. Add a Campden tablet and let sit, covered, for 24 hours. Make a yeast starter-culture by combining the champagne yeast and yeast nutrient with 1 1/2 cups tepid orange juice. Cover, shake vigorously, and let stand until bubbly (1–3 hours); then add to the must. Add acid blend (or citrus juice) and enough water to make 1 gallon. Cover loosely. Ferment for 3 days. Rack. Ferment for an additional 10 days and rack again. Transfer to a 1-gallon airlocked vessel and allow the wine to complete the fermentation process. Bottle, cork, and cellar the wine. Wait at least 6 months before opening a bottle.

Apple Melomel

Also known as cyser or applejack-honey wine, this is an old, old wine, popular in Europe long before pioneer families made it and it became the stuff of country-and-western music. Part of its historic popularity can surely be attributed to the availability of apples in fall gardens and the chance finding of "bee trees." It takes pedestrian hard cider into the realm of fine wines by touching it with the subtle honey essence that is key to its flavor. Be sure to use fresh cider, without preservatives that will inhibit the fermentation process.

3 pounds honey
1 gallon apple cider
1 Campden tablet (optional)
1 teaspoon acid blend *or* the juice of 1 lemon and 2
   oranges
1 package champagne yeast (5–7 grams)
1 teaspoon yeast nutrient
1½ cups orange juice

Combine the honey and cider in a non-aluminum pan. Boil for 15 minutes and skim off the foam. Pour into a 2-gallon plastic container when the mixture has cooled. Add a Campden tablet, if desired, and let the mixture sit, covered, for 24 hours. Add the acid blend (or citrus juices). Make a yeast starter-culture by combining the champagne yeast and yeast nutrient with 1½ cups tepid orange juice. Cover, shake vigorously, and let stand until bubbly (1–3 hours); then add to the must. Ferment for 5 days. Rack. Ferment for 10 more days. Rack again. Store in a 1-gallon airlocked container until the fermentation is complete. Bottle, cork, and cellar the wine. Wait 6 months before sampling.

GRAPE MELOMEL

This fine country wine has an ancient history. Known as pymeat, *it was popular in ancient Egypt.*

3 pounds light honey
3 pounds Concord grapes
1 Campden tablet (optional)
1 package champagne yeast (5–7 grams)
1 teaspoon yeast nutrient
1½ cups orange juice
1 teaspoon pectic enzyme

Remove the impurities from the honey by boiling 1 part honey with 2 parts water in a large, non-aluminum pot and skimming off the foam. Cool. Put the grapes into a 2-gallon plastic container and crush. Add the honey-and-water mixture, adding extra water to make 1 gallon if necessary. You may add a Campden tablet to kill off any wild yeasts that are present, if desired, since grapes usually have wild yeasts on their skins. Let the mixture stand for 24 hours, well covered, stirring two or three times in an up-and-down motion to introduce oxygen into the mixture. Make a yeast starter-culture by combining the champagne yeast and yeast nutrient with 1 1/2 cups tepid orange juice. Cover, shake vigorously, and let stand until bubbly (1–3 hours); then add to the must. Add the pectic enzyme. Ferment for 5 days and strain out the solids. Transfer the liquid to an airlocked vessel. Rack after 2 weeks. When all fermentation has ceased, bottle the wine. Wait 6 months or more before opening a bottle.

ROSE HIP MELOMEL

If you are lucky enough to have a rose garden containing the old rugosa shrub roses that have been popular in the United States almost since its beginning, you'll have the perfect source of rose hips for this delicious wine. Rose hips are the fruit of the rose bush; they have a taste reminiscent of apples and are a natural source of vitamin C. The best source of rose hips is the rugosa rose — a favorite of this country's pioneers, who hadn't the time or the inclination to coddle wimpy roses. They planted rugosas to add a touch of delicate beauty to their landscapes, but the variety proved to be so tough that many of the roses outlived their gardeners.

While hiking in the Smoky Mountains, we once came upon an abandoned cabin completely surrounded with rugosa roses. We couldn't even get through the barrier they created. Finding so many plump, red-orange rose hips there for the taking, we left our hike for another day and enthusiastically gathered the bounty into jackets-turned-tote-bags.

If you get your rose hips from more dandified roses, be careful of the source. So many of today's pampered hybrid teas are treated with a variety of chemicals — some of them systemic insecticides that remain in the plant tissues — that they are scarcely a food source. Even if you are sure of your source, be sure to wash the hips thoroughly. Even untreated roses are likely to be in locations where environmental pollutants are common.

This is a very sweet wine, good for desserts or as an after-dinner drink. We like to mix it with iced tea for a deliciously different, refreshing summer cooler. You can also combine it with orange juice and a lemon-lime soft drink, like Seven-Up, for one of the best, and most unusual, wine coolers you've ever tasted.

3¼ pounds honey
1 orange (bitter is best)
4 pounds rose hips
1 Campden tablet (optional)
1 package champagne yeast (5–7 grams)
1 teaspoon yeast nutrient
1½ cups orange juice
1 tablespoon acid blend *or* the juice of 1 lemon and 2
   oranges
1 teaspoon pectic enzyme

Remove impurities from the honey by boiling it with water (1 part honey to 2 parts water) in a large, non-aluminum saucepan, skimming off any foam that rises to the top. Grate the orange, making sure to use only the outer rind, not the bitter, white inner rind. In another large, non-aluminum pan, boil the rose hips and orange rind in about ³/₄ gallon of water until the hips are fork tender. Strain out the solids (discard them). When the two liquids have cooled, add the honey-water mixture and the liquor from the rose hips to a 2-gallon plastic container. Add a Campden tablet, if desired, and let the mixture sit, covered, for 24 hours. Then add the acid blend and the pectic enzyme. Make a yeast starter-culture by combining the champagne yeast and yeast nutrient with 1½ cups tepid orange juice. Cover, shake vigorously, and let stand until bubbly (1–3 hours); then add to the must. Allow the mixture to rest for 10 days, loosely covered. Then rack into a 1-gallon airlocked fermentation vessel and let it ferment for about 3 months. When the fermentation is complete, rack, bottle, cork, and cellar the wine, waiting at least 6 months to sample.

TANGERINE MELOMEL

3 pounds honey
Juice and rind of 2 sweet oranges
1 12-ounce can frozen tangerine-juice concentrate
Juice of 1 lemon
1 teaspoon pectic enzyme
1 Campden tablet (optional)
1 package champagne yeast (5–7 grams)
1 teaspoon yeast nutrient
1½ cups orange juice

Boil the honey with 2 parts water to 1 part honey in a large, non-aluminum saucepan for about 15 minutes, skimming the foam from the top of the mixture. When no more foam rises to the top, transfer to a 2-gallon plastic container and add the grated orange rind. Let the mixture cool and add the tangerine-juice concentrate, lemon juice, orange juice, and pectic enzyme. Add water to make 1 gallon. If you wish to eliminate wild yeasts, add a Campden tablet at this time and let the mixture sit, well covered, for 24 hours before proceeding. Make a yeast starter-culture by combining the champagne yeast and yeast nutrient with 1½ cups tepid orange juice. Cover, shake vigorously, and let stand until bubbly (1–3 hours); then add to the must.

Ferment until you can no longer hear it bubbling; then rack into a 1-gallon airlocked fermentation vessel and ferment for 3 months. Rack as needed to clear the wine. Fermentation should be complete in about 6 months. When you're sure it's complete, rack the wine into bottles, cork, and store for at least 6 months before sampling.

STRAWBERRY MELOMEL

Sweet and so delicious it's almost sinful, this honey-strawberry combination seems to preserve the delicate strawberry flavor better than other, conventional strawberry wines.

    3 pounds strawberries
    1 Campden tablet (optional)
    3 pounds clover honey
    1 package champagne yeast (5–7 grams)
    1 teaspoon yeast nutrient
    1½ cups orange juice
    1 teaspoon acid blend *or* the juice of H lemon
    1 teaspoon pectic enzyme

Put berries into a 2-gallon plastic container and crush. Add a Campden tablet, if desired, and let the mixture sit, covered, for 24 hours. Boil the honey with water, 2 parts water to 1 part honey, in a large, non-aluminum pot. Skim off foam and cool. Make a yeast starter-culture by combining the champagne yeast and yeast nutrient with 1½ cups tepid orange juice. Cover, shake vigorously, and let stand until bubbly (1–3 hours); then add to the must. Add the acid blend, pectic enzyme, and enough water to make 1 gallon. Let stand for 24 hours, stirring two or three times at intervals. Ferment for 3 days. Rack. Ferment for 10 more days and rack again. Transfer the liquid to a 1-gallon airlocked fermentation vessel and allow to ferment to completion. Bottle, cork, and cellar the wine. Difficult as it may be, wait at least 6 months before sampling.

MAKING METHEGLINS

Metheglins, honey-based wines in which the flavor is augmented by herbs or spices, are as varied as the people who make them. Some truly fine wines with excellent bouquets result from fermenting honey with herbs or spices. The list of metheglins is never complete. They may be simple, consisting of a single herb combined with honey, water, and yeast, and appropriate nutrients, or they may be complex with a multitude of ingredients.

The wines made from honey and herbs or spices stimulate the palate as drinks, but they really come into their own as cooking wines — imparting their subtle charm to recipes that many of us may have tasted and tried in vain to duplicate.

Our friends often talk about the flavor of our annual Christmas-party turkey, which we baste and inject with natural mead and stuff with a traditional stuffing augmented with sage metheglin and natural mead. (The recipe for this unusually delicious treatment of a traditional holiday favorite is on page 105 in the chapter on cooking with wines.)

If you've tried honey glazes for hams or fowl — or even a whole roasted salmon — and found the honey flavor too strong for your taste, metheglins might change your mind about honey in cooking. The honey and herbs in metheglins are always subtle, never overpowering. The wines seem to penetrate the meat, fowl, and fish with subtle flavors that may earn you a reputation as the best cook in town. These wines, should you be willing to part with them to make honey-herbal vinegars, also give an entirely new dimension to salad dressings and marinades. (We'll tell you more about that in the chapter on making vinegars from homemade wines, page 120.)

To acquaint you with some of the possibilities that exist for making metheglins, we have prepared a list of herbs and spices used in these wines. The list is by no means exhaustive — we urge you to experiment. Just be sure to check the properties of the herb before you make a metheglin from it. Hayfever sufferers, for example, might be well advised to stay away from camomile metheglin, which contains an herb from the same botanical family as ragweed — the less flavorful branch of the family tree. Camomile tea has long been recommended as a relaxing bedtime beverage, but if you become not only relaxed but also stuffy-nosed when you drink it, don't even be tempted by camomile metheglin — though its slightly perfumey bouquet is tantalizing.

The amounts of the flavoring components used in metheglins depend on the nature of the wine and the use you intend for it. If you are in doubt, start by making a fairly strong tea from the herb you want to try and then make the tea into a honey-based wine. For cooking wines, you may need slightly stronger tea. Metheglins are short on effort and long on flavor. And there is a great variety in the kinds of herbs and spices used for metheglins. Depending on growing conditions, herbs vary widely in the strength of the flavorful essential oils that account for their taste. Treat herbs well, giving them fertilizer and plenty of water, and they are likely to be milder and *less* flavorful than herbs grown in poor, dry soil.

METHEGLIN FLAVORINGS

tarragon(French)	sweet marjoram	peppermint
stick cinnamon	rosemary	mace
nutmeg	whole cloves	orange peel
balm	lemon peel	hyssop
rose petals	camomile	lemon mint
ginger	sweet basil	sage
sweet woodruff	cardamom	fennel root
spearmint	orange mint	honeysuckle
thymes	lemon balm	angelica
caraway seeds	parsley	violet
clover blossom	almonds	dandelions
vanilla	juniper berries	orange blossoms

PROPORTION OF FLAVORING INGREDIENTS

Dried herbs	2–3 ounces per gallon
Fresh herbs	2–4 pints per gallon, loosely packed
Nuts	1–2 ounces per gallon
Cinnamon sticks	1–3 sticks per gallon
Juniper berries	4–5 per gallon (juniper berries are one of the flavoring components of gin — a few go a long way)
Rinds (citrus)	2–3 fruits per gallon (just the outer rind, not the white inner rind)

Before we give you some of our favorite recipes, examine the list of metheglin flavorings on page 64 to gauge just a few of the possibilities.

Since neither the honey nor the herbs and spices in metheglins provide the necessary nutrients for full fermentation, older metheglin recipes usually include a couple of oranges and a lemon or some other citrus fruit. Sometimes the citrus seems to enhance the flavor of the herb or spice. When we don't want to add citrus, we usually just add yeast nutrients to metheglins. When you are ready to develop your own metheglins, think about the flavors you like and vary the ingredients accordingly. Just remember, if you use yeast nutrient instead of citrus fruits, you'll also need to add acid blend to provide the acid component needed in your wine.

To help you develop your own special metheglins, the table on this page will help you with the correct proportions of the flavoring ingredients. Dried herbs have a much more intense flavor than fresh herbs; the drying process reduces the volume but not the flavor.

Since the amounts of flavoring components used to make metheglins can vary according to taste, should you find the flavor too strong, simply blend the metheglin with other vintages of meads or melomels until you have adjusted the metheglin to the subtle flavor characteristics that suit your taste. You can also mix metheglins with fruit wines and fruit juices to make exciting wine coolers with a special taste produced by your own secret set of ingredients.

PROPORTION OF NUTRIENT INGREDIENTS

Grapes, fresh	2 pounds per gallon
Raisins	1 pound per gallon
Grape concentrate	1/2 pint per gallon
Grape juice	32 fluid ounces per gallon
Citrus fruits	3 per gallon
Other fruits	Varies to taste, usually 1–2 pounds per gallon
Yeast nutrient	1 teaspoon per gallon (or follow supplier's directions)
Acid blend	1/2 to 1 1/2 teaspoons per gallon (or follow supplier's directions)

Of all the wines we researched and developed, we think metheglins are the most exciting. If you've already discovered the ease and pleasure of growing herbs in your garden (or in pots on the windowsill), using herbs in winemaking is a natural outgrowth of your cooking experiments with Mother Nature's seasonings.

Herbal wines and meads have been made by monks for centuries. And the secret and solitary nature of their activities gives metheglins their historical mystique. Maybe the next chartreuse has already been created in the kitchen of some amateur winemaker who experimented with herbs from his backyard garden. If you aren't quite ready for that distinction, start by trying some of these recipes for metheglins.

GINGER METHEGLIN

This metheglin is a superb component of a ginger-flavored marinade (see page 114) for chicken or duck in Oriental dishes. The ginger flavor is subtle, not overpowering as it sometimes is in such dishes. Or use this metheglin in a delicious ginger-flavored wine cooler — a little like ginger ale with an adult flair. Just mix lime juice, ginger metheglin, and seltzer or a lemon-lime soda and pour it over crushed ice. It's a delightfully cooling summer beverage.

3 pounds honey
3 ounces whole ginger root, bruised
1 orange
1 lemon
1 lime
1 Campden tablet (optional)
$1/2$ pint white grape-juice concentrate
1 package champagne yeast (5–7 grams)
1 teaspoon yeast nutrient
$1 1/2$ cups orange juice

Prepare the honey by boiling it with water, 1 part honey to 2 parts water, in a large, non-aluminum pot. (You can use the empty honey jar to measure the water.) Skim off the foam; remove from the heat when no more foam rises to the top. Add the bruised ginger and cool. Juice the citrus fruits and grate the outer rinds (avoiding the white inner rind) and add the juice and grated rind to the mixture. Transfer to a 2-gallon plastic container. Add a Campden tablet, if desired, and let the mixture sit, well covered, for 24 hours. Then add the juice concentrate and enough water to make a gallon. Make a yeast starter-culture by combining the champagne yeast and yeast nutrient with $1 1/2$ cups tepid orange juice. Cover, shake vigorously, and let stand until bubbly (1–3 hours); then add to the must. Allow the mixture to stand for 24 hours, loosely covered, stirring two or three times at intervals. Rack into a 1-gallon airlocked fermentation vessel and allow to ferment to completion. Rack into bottles, cork, and cellar. Wait 6 months or more before sampling.

ROSE PETAL METHEGLIN

This wine is reminiscent of the Egyptian delicacy, rosewater, and it can be used in many Middle Eastern recipes that call for rosewater. The rose flavor is so delicate and so delicious, however, and the pale pink color (if you use red rose petals) so delightful in cut-glass wineglasses that we'll bet you reserve this wine for extra special occasions. It's a perfect accompaniment for light desserts or light, nutty cheeses.

2 1/2 pounds honey
2 quarts loosely packed rose petals
1 lemon
3/4 pound light raisins *or* 1 pint white grape-juice concentrate
1 orange
1 Campden tablet (optional)
1 package champagne yeast (5–7 grams)
1 teaspoon yeast nutrient
1 1/2 cups orange juice

Boil the honey and water — 1 part honey to 2 parts water — for about 15 minutes in a large, non-aluminum pot and skim off the white foam that forms on top. (You can use the empty honey jar to measure the water.) Cool. Combine the cooled honey with the next four ingredients and enough water to make a gallon in a 2-gallon plastic container. Add a Campden tablet, if desired, and let stand for 24 hours, loosely covered, stirring two or three times at intervals. Make a yeast starter-culture by combining the champagne yeast and yeast nutrient with 1 1/2 cups tepid orange juice. Cover, shake vigorously, and let stand until bubbly (1–3 hours); then add to the must. Rack into a 1-gallon airlocked fermentation vessel and let it ferment to completion, racking as needed to clarify the wine. When fermentation is complete and the wine is clear, bottle, cork, and cellar the wine. Wait at least 6 months before sampling.

TARRAGON METHEGLIN

This wine tastes a bit like licorice or a mild anisette and makes a good addition to cookies and candies, as well as fish and chicken dishes.

1 lemon
3 pounds honey
3 ounces dried tarragon *or* 1 quart fresh tarragon,
    loosely packed
3 ounces frozen tangerine-juice concentrate
1/2 pound light raisins
1 Campden tablet (optional)
1 package champagne yeast (5–7 grams)
1 teaspoon yeast nutrient
1 1/2 cups orange juice
1 teaspoon pectic enzyme

Remove the rind from the lemon with a vegetable peeler or grater, being careful not to include any of the bitter, white inner rind. Set the grated rind aside. Boil the honey with water (2 parts water to 1 part honey) for about 15 minutes in a large, non-aluminum pot, skimming off the foam that rises to the top. (You can use the empty honey jar to measure the water.) When the foam stops rising, remove the mixture from the heat and add the lemon rind. Allow the mixture to cool and transfer it to a 2-gallon plastic container. Juice the lemon and add the lemon juice, tarragon, tangerine concentrate, raisins, and enough water to make a gallon. Add a Campden tablet, if desired, and let the mixture sit, covered, for 24 hours before proceeding. Make a yeast starter-culture by combining the champagne yeast and yeast nutrient with 1½ cups tepid orange juice. Cover, shake vigorously, and let stand until bubbly (1–3 hours); then add to the must. Add the pectic enzyme. Cover loosely. Stir the mixture two or three times at intervals over the next 24 hours. When the first fermentation is complete, rack the wine into a 1-gallon airlocked fermentation vessel and let it ferment to completion. When the wine has cleared and fermentation is complete, bottle, cork, and cellar the wine. Wait at least 6 months before sampling for best flavor.

Lemon-Thyme Metheglin

Lemon-thyme metheglin adds a whole new dimension to poached salmon when it's added to the poaching liquids; we've used lemon-thyme-metheglin vinegar as a component of a delectable dressing for a salmon salad. It's equally good for dressing up such standard fare as tuna or chicken salad. You'll never eat better!

3 pounds honey
1 pint fresh lemon thyme, loosely packed
1 lemon
3 ounces frozen tangerine-juice concentrate
½ pound light raisins
1 Campden tablet (optional)
1 package champagne yeast (5–7 grams)
1 teaspoon yeast nutrient
1½ cups orange juice

Boil the honey and water — 2 parts water to 1 part honey — for about 15 minutes in a large, non-aluminum pot and skim off the white foam that forms on top. (You can use the empty honey jar to measure the water.) Cool. Add the cooled honey to the next four ingredients, with enough water to make a gallon, in a 2-gallon plastic container. Add a Campden tablet, if desired, and let stand for 24 hours, loosely covered, stirring two or three times at intervals. Make a yeast starter-culture by combining the champagne yeast and yeast nutrient with 1½ cups tepid orange juice. Cover, shake vigorously, and let stand until bubbly (1–3 hours); then add to the must. Rack into a 1-gallon airlocked fermentation vessel and allow to ferment to completion, racking as needed to clarify the wine. When fermentation is complete and the wine has achieved sufficient clarity, bottle, cork, and cellar the wine. Wait at least 6 months before sampling.

5

Herbal Wines

Wines made with herbs and spices are often among the most complex and sophisticated wines in the cellar, not because they are more difficult to make, but because the flavors encompass a whole range of sensations — from strong and assertive to soft and so subtle as to be almost subliminal. Many draw their flavors from a blending of the herb or spice with the complex flavors of grape or honey wines, either of which makes a fine base for herbal wines.

No wine that you make will bear your signature more clearly than those with herbs and spices as the major flavoring component. But before you begin to blend these highly individual wines, you do need some basic understanding of the role of the grape in this exciting alchemy.

For the winemaker, three main classes of grapes are important: labruscas, which include the Delaware, Catawba, and Concord; vinifera grapes, which produce the fine wines of Europe, such as Cabernet Sauvignon, Sémillon, and Merlot; and the French hybrids, which are grown in wide-ranging areas of the United States and include such varieties as Vignoles, Banco Noir, and the Seyval Blanc. Making wine from this wide array of grapes can be very simple or very complex.

Consistently great grape wines happen only when the vintner is blessed with a good crop and knows how to treat it correctly.

There are, however, some underlying principles that can help you produce good and sometimes even great wines. (The difference between good and great wines is very subjective, and once we get away from the notion that only wines praised by experts can qualify, you may find that your homemade wine has an edge. After all, it is custom made to suit your individual taste.)

From the three classes of grapes listed above come all the red, white, and pink (also called *blush* or *rosé*) wines that we're used to seeing in wine stores. Red wines are, generally speaking, created from a red or purple grape variety whose skins are crushed along with the grapes and left in the must during the first fermentation. It is the skin on the grape that gives color to the wine, and the skins are also the source of natural yeasts that make it possible to ferment grape juice into wine without the addition of commercial yeasts (although most winemakers would rather add the yeast so they're sure of what they'll be getting). This marriage of yeast and grape probably accounted for wine's discovery in the first place — undoubtedly by some country dweller whose chance use of the juice from spoiled grapes started today's winemaking tradition.

If the skins of a purple or red grape are removed and left out of the first fermentation, the resulting wine will be white, regardless of the color of grape used. White Concord wines are fermented this way. White grape varieties with white skins (what we commonly call green or golden grapes) produce white wine with or without the skins.

White wines, then, differ from red wines because either they have been fermented without the skins or they have white skins to begin with, which do not give color to the finished wine. Too, white wines usually get racked one additional time before they are fitted with a fermentation lock for the second fermentation. For that reason their flavors are often fresher than those of red wines.

We'll give you some of the recipes we've tried and liked in this chapter, but we'd also like to encourage you to try some of your own recipes. To get you started, we'll give you a basic recipe for Herb or Dried-Flower-Petal Wine (page 74), a white wine. This recipe has only two variations. The first decision you'll need to make is whether to use grapes or raisins. If you decide on raisins, use 1 pound of light raisins and the necessary water to make 1 gallon. If you decide on grapes, use the juice of 3½–4 pounds of grapes and water to make 1 gallon. (Either use white grapes or omit the skins to ensure that you'll have a white wine base.) The second decision is which of the many herbs, flowers, and spices to use to flavor your wine. Any of the flowers and herbs listed under Flavoring Components for White Herbal Wines below can be added in the amount of 2 ounces, as long as they are *dried*. Later on, as you gain more experience, you'll probably vary the amounts somewhat to suit your own tastes. (If you use fresh herbs or petals, you'll need to increase the amount to 1–4 pints, depending on your taste and the strength of the herb or flower flavor.)

White Herbal Wines

cowslip flowers	lemon balm	burnet
elderflowers	rosemary	bramble tips
comfrey root	rose petals	dandelion
coltsfoot	rhubarb	agrimony
coltsfoot flowers		

Red Wines

cinnamon sticks
cardamom seeds
whole cloves
ginger root

Herbal Meads

rosemary	sweet basil	cinnamon sticks
rose petals	hyssop	ground mace
camomile	sweet woodruff	whole nutmeg
lemon mint	cardamom seeds	whole cloves
thyme	lemon balm	marjoram
parsley roots	caraway seeds	rose hips
fennel roots	citrus peel	ginger root

To create more robust wines with an herb or spice component, you may substitute dark raisins for light or use red, purple, or black grapes and include the skins in the must. If you include the grape skins, you'll have a red wine. See page 73 for some possible herbs and spices for use in red wines. The list of herbal meads is long and tantalizing. Using the basic mead recipe (page 53) in the chapter on honey wines, you can experiment with adding 2 ounces of the dried herbs and spices on page 73. Finally, apéritif wines can be created by adding wormwood (to produce a vermouth or absinthe flavor), anise seeds (to produce a Pernod flavor), or globe artichokes (to produce an Italian Cynar flavor).

While you are deciding on your own contribution to the herbal wine field, here are some herbal wines that we've tried and liked. Some we use as delightfully different after-dinner beverages, others make refreshing wine coolers or spritzers, or turn ordinary iced tea into a celebration.

HERB OR DRIED-FLOWER-PETAL WINE

A surprising number of delicious wines come from flower petals. The recipe we've included here is a general one, so you may substitute any of your favorite herbs or edible flowers. A word of caution: Whenever you use flowers in wine or cooking, make sure that they come from edible plants. The lovely oleander bloom is deadly, as are the flowers of lily of the valley. A good rule to follow is, if you aren't sure, don't use it. (See page 154 for more about this.)

> 2 ounces *dried* herbs or flower petals
> 1 pound minced sultanas or other light raisins *or* juice of
>   3½–4 pounds grapes
> 1 teaspoon citric acid *or* 2 teaspoons acid blend
> 1 teaspoon tannin
> 1 Campden tablet (optional)
> 1 package wine yeast (5–7 grams)
> 1 teaspoon yeast nutrient
> 1½ cups orange juice
> 2¼ pounds sugar for dry wines, 2¾ pounds for sweet

Place the dried herbs or flower petals in an enamel or glass saucepan with 1 quart of water. Bring the mixture to a boil and simmer for about 20 minutes. Transfer to a 2-gallon plastic container and add the raisins, citric acid, and tannin. When the mixture is cool, add a Campden tablet, if desired, and let the mixture sit, covered, for 24 hours. Make a yeast starter-culture by combining the wine yeast and yeast nutrient with 1½ cups tepid orange juice. Cover, shake vigorously, and let stand until bubbly (1–3 hours); then add to the must. Ferment the pulp for 3 days, loosely covered. Then strain out the solids or rack the liquid into a 1-gallon fermentation vessel that can be fitted with an airlock. Add the desired amount of sugar and water to make 1 gallon. Fit the airlock, and let the wine ferment to completion. When you're sure the fermentation has stopped, bottle, cork, and cellar the wine.

LEMON-THYME WINE

2¼ pounds rhubarb
1 pint fresh lemon-thyme leaves
2 pounds raisins *or* ½ pint white grape-juice concentrate
1 Campden tablet (optional)
1 package wine yeast (5–7 grams)
1 teaspoon yeast nutrient
1½ cups orange juice
2¼ pounds sugar

Cut the rhubarb into ½-inch slices, chop the lemon thyme, and put both ingredients in a large glass or plastic container. Bring 3½ quarts of water to a boil and pour it over the thyme and rhubarb. Then add the raisins or grape concentrate. Add a Campden tablet, if desired. Let the mixture sit, loosely covered, stirring occasionally, for 2 weeks. Make a yeast starter-culture by combining the wine yeast and yeast nutrient with 1½ cups tepid orange juice. Cover, shake vigorously, and let stand until bubbly (1–3 hours); then add to the must. Put the sugar in a second 2-gallon plastic container and strain or rack the mixture onto the sugar. Add water to make a gallon, if needed. Cover the container loosely and wait for about 2 more weeks. Then rack the mixture into a 1-gallon airlocked fermentation vessel and let the wine ferment to completion.

Note: If you prefer a sweeter wine, you can increase the sugar by $1/2$ to 1 pound. Just taste the wine and adjust accordingly. If you add additional sugar once the original fermentation is complete, let the wine sit in the fermentation vessel for an additional 2 to 4 weeks before you bottle it, in case the additional sugar triggers another fermentation. When you're sure that the wine is fermented out, bottle, cork, and cellar the wine. Wait 6 months or more before opening a bottle.

SWEET PARSLEY WINE

1 quart coarsely chopped fresh parsley
2 oranges
7 cups sugar
2 tablespoons lemon juice
3 cloves
1 Campden tablet (optional)
1 package wine yeast (5–7 grams)
1 teaspoon yeast nutrient
$1 1/2$ cups orange juice

Wash the parsley and grate just the outer rind of the oranges (a vegetable peeler works well), avoiding the bitter, white inner rind. Then squeeze the juice from the oranges and set it aside. Add the parsley and orange rind to a large glass or enamel container with $3^{1}/_{2}$ quarts of water and simmer for 30 minutes. Strain out the solids and pour the juices into a 2-gallon plastic wastebasket or bucket. When the mixture is cool, add the next three ingredients. Add a Campden tablet, if desired, and let the mixture sit, covered, for 24 hours before proceeding. Make a yeast starter-culture by combining the wine yeast and yeast nutrient with $1^{1}/_{2}$ cups tepid orange juice. Cover, shake vigorously, and let stand until bubbly (1–3 hours); then add to the must. Let the mixture sit in a warm place to ferment, loosely covered. After 11 days, strain the mixture into a 1-gallon airlocked fermentation vessel. After an additional 12 days have passed, rack into another 1-gallon, airlocked container and let the wine mature. Bottle after 1 year; then wait 6 months before sampling.

PARSLEY WINE

1 pound fresh parsley
2 oranges
2 lemons
1 teaspoon chopped ginger root
3 pounds sugar
1 Campden tablet (optional)
1 teaspoon grape tannin
1 package wine yeast (5–7 grams)
1 teaspoon yeast nutrient
1 1/2 cups orange juice

Prepare your freshly picked parsley by running cold water over it in a colander or strainer and chopping it coarsely. Then grate the outer rind of the citrus fruits, using a vegetable peeler so that you don't get any of the bitter, white inner rind. Boil the parsley, orange and lemon rind, and the ginger in 3 1/2 quarts of water for 20–30 minutes in a large enamel or stainless steel pot. Squeeze the juice from the fruits and then strain the juices onto the sugar in a 2-gallon plastic wastebasket or bucket. Let the mixture cool. Add a Campden tablet, if desired, and let the mixture sit, covered, for 24 hours. Then add the tannin and water to make a gallon if needed. Make a yeast starter-culture by combining the wine yeast and yeast nutrient with 1 1/2 cups tepid orange juice. Cover, shake vigorously, and let stand until bubbly (1–3 hours); then add to the must. Let the mixture ferment for about 10 days with only a loose cover. Then rack into a 1-gallon airlocked fermentation vessel and let the mixture ferment to completion, racking as needed for clarity. Keep the mixture in the airlocked container for at least 6 months. Parsley wines need to be mature before you bottle them. Then bottle, cork, and cellar the wine. Wait several additional months before you sample it, so that the wine loses its "green" taste.

SAGE WINE I

Since a little sage goes a long way as far as we are concerned, we were surprised to discover numerous recipes for sage wines. We've always thought sage wines were at their best in the kitchen, where they complement poultry dishes like no other wine (except a sage metheglin). But the popularity of sage wine recipes leads us to think that many country winemakers found it equally satisfying in the dining room, perhaps as an apéritif. This recipe is typical of most of the recipes we found. The following one adds a couple of extra ingredients that make it truly unique. You may want to try both to see which you prefer.

> 2 limes
> 3–4 quarts loosely packed fresh sage leaves
> 1 pound light raisins
> 4 pounds sugar
> 1 Campden tablet (optional)
> 1 package wine yeast (5–7 grams)
> 1 teaspoon yeast nutrient
> 1 1/2 cups orange juice

Grate the outer rind of the limes, avoiding the white inner rind, and squeeze the juice from the limes. Put the sage leaves, raisins, and the juice and grated rind from the limes into a 2-gallon plastic wastebasket or bucket. Bring 1 quart of water to a boil and pour it over the ingredients in the bucket. Let the mixture sit for 2 or 3 hours, covered loosely. Then boil half the sugar in a quart of water for 2 minutes and add it to the mixture. When the mixture has cooled, add the Campden tablet, if desired, and let it stand 24 hours, well covered, before proceeding. (If you don't add a Campden tablet, you may continue immediately.) Make a yeast starter-culture by combining the wine yeast and yeast nutrient with 1 1/2 cups tepid orange juice. Cover, shake vigorously, and let stand until bubbly (1–3 hours); then add to the must. Allow the mixture to ferment, loosely covered, for 10 days, stirring daily. Then rack the wine into a 1-gallon airlocked fermentation vessel, discarding the solids. Boil the remaining sugar in a quart of water and when it has cooled add it to the fermentation vessel with additional water if needed to make a gallon. Allow the wine to ferment to completion, but taste it before you bottle. If the sage taste is too strong, dilute the wine with water to taste and add 3 to 4 ounces more sugar per pint of wine. Then let it sit in the airlocked fermentation vessel for another month before you bottle, cork, and cellar the wine. Wait 6 months or more before you open a bottle.

SAGE WINE II

> 2 lemons
> 3 ounces dried sage
> 1 pound light raisins
> 1 ounce dried mint
> 1 pound wheat berries
> 2½ pounds sugar
> 1 Campden tablet (optional)
> 1 package wine yeast (5–7 grams)
> 1 teaspoon yeast nutrient
> 1½ cups orange juice

Grate the outer rind of the lemons, avoiding the white inner rind, and squeeze the juice from the lemons. Put the sage, raisins, mint, wheat berries, and the rind and juice of the lemons in a 2-gallon plastic container and pour 1 quart of boiling water over the mixture. Cover loosely and let it stand for 2 to 3 hours. Boil half the sugar in a quart of water for 2 minutes and add to the liquor. Add a Campden tablet, if desired, and let sit for 24 hours, well covered, before proceeding. Make a yeast starter-culture by combining the wine yeast and yeast nutrient with 1½ cups tepid orange juice. Cover, shake vigorously, and let stand until bubbly (1–3 hours); then add to the must. Allow it to ferment for 10 days, stirring daily. Boil the remaining sugar in a quart of water and cool. Add the sugar-water solution, and additional water to make a gallon if needed, to a 1-gallon airlocked fermentation vessel and either rack or strain the liquor into the vessel, stirring to mix. Affix an airlock and allow the wine to ferment to completion. Then taste the wine. If it's too strong, dilute with water and add 3–4 ounces of sugar per pint of wine. Let the wine sit in the airlocked container for an additional 30 days. Tasting is necessary because the herbs vary considerably in strength, depending on where they were grown and how they were dried. Once you're sure of the taste and the fermentation is complete, bottle, cork, and cellar the wine. Wait 6 months or more before opening your first bottle.

6

Wine Coolers and Wine Punches

Nothing says "party" as effectively as luscious punches and wine coolers, but the search for really unusual punches is every host's headache. Something magic happens when your party punch is unique, derived from wines no other cellar can match. We had a grand time experimenting with the punches and coolers in this chapter — and there was never a shortage of people who volunteered to come to a tasting party!

ICED TEA COOLER

Iced tea takes on a whole new personality when you include it in this deliciously different cooler.

> 1 cup mead of your choice (pages 53–55)
> 6 cups strong tea
> 1 6-ounce can frozen lemonade concentrate
> 2 cans cold water
> 1 25-ounce bottle Lemon-Thyme Metheglin (page 69)
> Sprigs of fresh mint to garnish

Mix all the ingredients except the garnish and chill. Serve over crushed ice with the mint garnish. Makes approximately sixteen 6-ounce servings.

TROPICAL WINE PUNCH

For an unforgettable luau or tropical pool party, serve this easy-to-make punch from a bowl surrounded with red canna blossoms and make it the centerpiece of your buffet table. It's also luscious served in coconut cups — just drill a couple of large holes in each coconut, drain the liquid out, and fill with punch (a turkey baster or a funnel makes it easy). Garnish with fruit on a skewer and serve with a colorful drinking straw.

    1 46-ounce can Hawaiian Punch
    $^1/_4$ cup sugar
    $^1/_2$ cup brandy
    1 25-ounce bottle Strawberry Wine (page 30) or Strawberry Melomel (page 62)
    2 1-liter bottles seltzer or lemon-lime soda
    Orange slices to garnish
    Strawberries to garnish

Mix all the ingredients except the soda and garnishes and chill. When you're ready to serve the punch, add the soda and garnish with orange slices and strawberry halves or slices. Makes approximately twenty-four 6-ounce servings.

STRAWBERRY WINE PUNCH

    1 cup sugar
    $^1/_2$ cup water
    2 cups Strawberry Wine (page 30)
    2 cups orange juice
    $^1/_2$ cup lemon juice
    1 cup fresh or frozen strawberries, crushed
    1 quart seltzer

Mix sugar and water and bring to a boil to make a syrup. Cool. Combine the syrup with the strawberry wine, the juices, and the crushed strawberries. Chill. Just before serving, pour into a punch bowl and slowly add in the seltzer. Serve immediately. Makes approximately fifteen 6-ounce servings.

BLACKBERRY SANGRIA

You've never had sangria like this! Our guests love it at holiday get-togethers — and any holiday will do. It really sparkles when served with a make-it-yourself assortment of Mexican foods.

1 gallon Sweet Port-Style Blackberry Wine (page 20)
1 quart orange juice
1 cup lemon juice
1/2 cup brandy
1/2 cup sugar (or to taste)
1 quart seltzer
2 oranges, thinly sliced
1 lemon, thinly sliced

Mix and chill wine, juices, brandy, and sugar. When you're ready to serve, pour into a punch bowl, add the seltzer, and garnish with the thinly sliced oranges and lemons. Makes approximately thirty-five 6-ounce servings.

PASSIONATE FRUIT PUNCH

1 25-ounce bottle Mead (page 53)
1 28-ounce bottle passion-fruit juice
2 64-ounce bottles orange juice
2 46-ounce cans pineapple juice (unsweetened)
6 ounces grenadine
2 8-ounce bottles Rose's lime juice
8 32-ounce bottles ginger ale

Mix all ingredients, chill, and serve in a punch bowl. Makes approximately sixty-five 6-ounce servings.

YULE GLOGG

We like to serve this glogg whenever guests trudge through the snow to visit. It's warm and spicy and filled with good homemade wine and good cheer. It's a traditional Christmas drink, so when the holidays near be sure to have some cherry melomel on hand for the best glogg you've ever served.

1 orange, juice and peels (in spirals or pieces)
1 lemon, juice and peels (in spirals or pieces)
$^3/_4$ cup sugar
8 whole cloves
2 teaspoons cinnamon
$^1/_2$ gallon Cherry Melomel (page 57)
$^1/_2$ quart brandy
1 cup Almond Wine (page 37)

Mix the first five ingredients and bring them to a boil, boiling for 5 minutes in a large pot. Remove from the heat and add the remaining ingredients. Reheat just to simmering and serve immediately.

If you want to keep this glogg hot — but not too hot, because alcohol evaporates at a relatively low temperature — fill the carafe of your automatic-drip coffeemaker with glogg, place three pennies on the hot plate the pot rests on, and turn on the coffeemaker. The pennies raise the glogg a bit above the hot plate, and keep it just warm enough for pleasant drinking. Makes approximately fourteen 6-ounce servings.

HOT CRANAPPLE PUNCH

1 quart cranberry juice
$^3/_4$ cup sugar
3 oranges, pierced with a fork
16 whole cloves
6 cinnamon sticks
1 teaspoon ground allspice
2 25-ounce bottles Sweet Apple Wine (page 18)
2 cups rum (optional)
1 teaspoon bitters (optional)

Heat the cranberry juice, sugar, oranges, and spices to boiling. Reduce heat and simmer for about 5 minutes. Then add the apple wine and the rum and bitters, if used. Simmer until piping hot and serve immediately. Makes approximately sixteen 6-ounce servings (with rum).

SHOOTING MIXTURE

Prepare Shooting Mixture ahead of time and keep a bottle in your wine cellar or liquor cabinet. Mixed with seltzer or a lemon-lime soft drink, it makes a deliciously different wine cooler. The alcohol content of this mixture is high, so mix — and consume — with caution.

> 3 pints Cherry Melomel (page 57)
> 1 1/2 pints cherry brandy
> 1 pint cognac

Mix all the ingredients in exactly the proportions given in the recipe. Shooting Mixture keeps well if it is stored in a cool, dark place. Makes approximately forty-four 2-ounce servings.

ORANGE CUP SPRITZER

> 4 ounces dry white wine (White Clover or Parsley
>   Wine, for example, pages 45 and 77)
> 4 ounces orange juice
> 1/2 ounce Cointreau or Grand Marnier
> Seltzer to fill the glass

Mix the white wine, orange juice, and Cointreau or Grand Marnier in a large collins glass with some cracked ice. Fill the glass with seltzer and stir gently. Makes a single serving.

POINSETTIA SPRITZER

> 3 ounces cranberry juice
> 1/2 ounce Triple Sec
> 3 ounces Strawberry Melomel (page 62)
> Seltzer or lemon-lime soft drink

Pre-chill all the ingredients, as well as a large champagne glass or brandy snifter that will hold about 8 ounces. Mix the cranberry juice, Triple Sec, and strawberry melomel in the glass; then fill it up with soda. Makes one serving.

GINGER WINE PUNCH

    1 pint apple cider
    1 pint grapefruit juice
    1 pint pineapple juice
    Juice of 1 lemon
    1 25-ounce bottle Dry Apple Wine (page 17)
    1 pint-bottle brandy or bourbon
    2 25-ounce bottles Dry Ginger Wine (page 42) or
        Ginger Metheglin (page 66)
    1 quart ginger ale or seltzer
    1 apple
    Honey or maple syrup to taste

Pre-chill all the ingredients except the honey or syrup and blend everything, except the apple, in a large punch bowl containing a molded ice ring or a large chunk of ice. Garnish with diced apple or very thin apple slices. Makes approximately thirty 6-ounce servings.

CRANBERRY SPARKLE PUNCH

    1 pint cranberry juice
    Juice of 1 grapefruit
    Juice of 1/2 lime
    1 cup Juniper Metheglin (see pages 63–66) or gin
    Sugar or honey to taste
    1–2 25-ounce bottles homemade mead to taste (page 53)
    1 liter seltzer
    Maraschino cherries to garnish
    Orange peel to garnish

Mix all ingredients, except the seltzer and garnishes, in a punch bowl containing a molded ice ring or a large cake of ice. Just before serving, add the seltzer and garnish with cherries and orange peel. Makes approximately twenty-four 6-ounce servings.

LAFAYETTE PUNCH

6 oranges, thinly sliced
1 cup confectioners' sugar
2 25-ounce bottles White Clover Wine (page 45),
   chilled
3 25-ounce bottles brut champagne, chilled

Cover the bottom of a punch bowl with orange slices and lay down a heavy coating of confectioners' sugar. Pour 1 bottle of clover wine carefully over the oranges and let ripen for 2 hours. Then add a cake of ice and pour in the other bottle of wine and the champagne. Serve immediately. Makes approximately twenty 6-ounce servings.

WINE COLLINS SPRITZER

4 ounces Sweet Port-Style Blackberry Wine (page 20)
1 lime
Lemon-lime soda
Maraschino cherry

Pour the wine into a large collins glass half-filled with cracked ice. Add a squeeze of lime and a twist of peel. Fill to the top with lemon-lime soda, stir, and garnish with a cherry. Makes one serving.

HONOLULU SURF SPRITZER

4 ounces pineapple juice
Juice of ½ lime
½ ounce Southern Comfort
3 ounces Mead (page 53)
Seltzer
Pineapple stick to garnish

Mix all liquid ingredients except the seltzer in a blender with cracked ice. Pour into a large collins glass and fill with seltzer. Stir and garnish with a pineapple stick. Makes one serving.

BASIC WINE COOLER

We like this basic wine cooler made with sweet parsley wine, but any white or golden wine is especially delicious served as a cooler. Honey wines bring unusual charm to even ordinary wine coolers — and don't forget those brilliant berry wines.

> 1/2 glass wine, such as Sweet Parsley Wine (page 76)
> 1/4 glass lemonade
> 1/4 glass Sprite

Pre-chill all ingredients, pour into a glass, and mix with a swizzle stick. Add ice if desired. Makes one serving.

FUZZY PEACH FIZZ

> Peach Wine (page 26)
> Orange juice
> Peach juice or fresh puréed peaches
> Lemon-lime soda
> Fresh peaches for garnish, sliced
> Sprig of fresh mint for garnish

Chill the peach wine, orange juice, peach juice or peaches, and the soda thoroughly. Fill a tall glass about a quarter full with peach wine (more or less to suit your taste). Add orange juice until the glass is about half full, then add peach juice or peach purée until the glass is three-quarters full. Top off with the lemon-lime soda to achieve the fizz. Garnish with peach slices and a sprig of fresh mint. This punch can be made by the pitcher for fizzy party fare. Makes any amount.

CRANBERRY SHRUB

If you add some puréed cranberries to this shrub, it makes a novel and delicious way to serve a traditional Thanksgiving favorite. Leave the wine out, add Seven-Up, and even the little ones can enjoy the delicious taste and lively color.

2 cups any berry wine (see Chapter 2)
1 pint cranberry juice cocktail
1 6-ounce can frozen pineapple-juice concentrate
Orange slices to garnish

Combine all the ingredients except the orange slices and pour over ice in a large pitcher. Stir to chill. Garnish each serving with an orange slice when you serve it up in clear glass punch cups. Makes approximately six 6-ounce servings.

BELLINI ROYAL PEACH PUNCH

3 ounces puréed ripe peaches
2 teaspoons lemon juice
Maraschino liqueur to taste
3 ounces Peach Wine (page 26)
Brut champagne or lemon-lime soda
Maraschino cherry to garnish
Peach slice to garnish

Chill a large goblet or brandy snifter in the freezer for about an hour before you make this punch. Sprinkle the puréed peaches with lemon juice and sweeten with the maraschino liqueur. Pour the purée into the chilled goblet and cover with peach wine. Then add the champagne and stir. (For a milder punch, use lemon-lime soda in place of champagne.) Garnish with a maraschino cherry and a peach slice. Makes one serving.

ORANGE COOLER

¼ glass Tangerine Melomel (page 61)
½ glass orange juice
¼ glass lemon-lime soda

Pre-chill all the ingredients. Pour wine and orange juice into a chilled glass or over ice and add the soda last. Makes one serving.

CHERRY COLA COOLER

> Cherry Melomel (page 57)
> Cola
> Orange slice
> Maraschino cherry

Fill a glass one-third to half full with cherry melomel. Then fill it the rest of the way with your choice of cola. Serve over crushed ice and garnish with an orange slice wrapped around a cherry on a toothpick. Cherry cola with punch! Makes any amount.

BASIL CUP

If sweet punches aren't high on your list of beverages, try this unusual concoction. It's great served with a salad and nut bread spread with cream cheese.

> 1 cup sweet basil leaves
> 1 25-ounce bottle any honey wine (see Chapter 4)
> Juice of 1 lemon
> Thin lemon slices for garnish

Wash a generous cup of fresh basil leaves, bruise them slightly to release the flavor, and steep them in honey wine for 3–4 hours. Strain out the basil leaves and pour the wine into a punch bowl, pitcher, or individual glasses. Add a dash or two of lemon juice to taste. Garnish with thinly sliced lemon, either floating in the punch bowl or decorating the glasses. Makes approximately six 6-ounce servings.

ROYAL RASPBERRY COOLER

So delicious it's almost dessert, this delightful punch not only tastes wonderfully like fresh raspberries, but it looks beautiful, too — in a decorated punch bowl or in clear glass punch cups.

1 quart raspberry sherbet or sorbet
1 25-ounce bottle Sweet Red Raspberry Wine (page 28)
½ 25-ounce bottle Tangerine Melomel (page 61)
1 cup orange juice
2 bottles champagne *or* 1 25-ounce bottle Mead (page
    53) and 1 liter bottle Sprite, chilled
1 cup fresh raspberries

Blend all the ingredients except the champagne and raspberries in a punch bowl and float an ice ring or mold in it. Just before serving, pour in the chilled champagne and stir gently. Garnish with fresh raspberries on a skewer or floated in the punch. Makes approximately twenty-two 6-ounce servings.

TROPICAL PUNCH

A takeoff on the famous Bengal Lancers' Rum Punch, this tropical drink takes on added dimensions when you use your own blackberry wine as a delightful flavoring component.

Juice of ½ lemon
½ cup orange juice
1 cup pineapple juice
½ cup lime juice
1 25-ounce bottle Blackberry Wine (page 19)
3 ounces light rum (optional)
Sugar to taste
1 25-ounce bottle champagne
8 ounces seltzer
Orange slices for garnish
Lime slices for garnish

Pre-chill all the liquid ingredients and mix everything except the champagne and seltzer and the orange and lime slices. Float an ice ring or other molded ice form in a punch bowl with the wine and rum and juices. Immediately before serving, add the champagne and seltzer gently, to preserve the bubbles. Garnish with thinly sliced oranges and limes. Makes approximately twelve 6-ounce servings.

Basic Wine Lemonade (Lemon Cooler)

This recipe works with almost any homemade wine, and each choice is an adventure — so experiment freely! Use a white wine for regular lemonade, a red or rosé for pink lemonade.

> **Juice of half a lemon**
> **Sugar to taste**
> **4 ounces dry or sweet wine — white, red, or rosé**
> **Seltzer**

Mix lemon juice, sugar, and wine in a collins glass with cracked ice. Stir until the sugar is dissolved and fill the glass with seltzer. Makes one serving.

7

Cooking with Country Wines

Cooking with wine can give you a lot of new twists for a variety of recipes, but if you've never used wine in cooking, the most likely place to start is with wine-based marinades. Later on in this chapter, we'll give you a few recipes for our favorite marinades — from a subtle, sweet Oriental one (page 114) to a zesty hot one for spicy Mexican dishes (page 115).

But wines are much too versatile to be limited to meat dishes alone. They also add their special flavors to appetizers, salads, vegetables, and even desserts. That's why each new recipe you try may suggest still other ways of using homemade country wines as a special ingredient in many of your family favorites.

Most of the time, the wines you use for cooking will be combined with foods that are heated to the point that alcohol evaporates — a lower temperature than the boiling point of water. What will remain with the food is flavor — flavor complex enough to take ordinary foods into the realm of haute cuisine.

We have included a few recipes for every phase of your dining experience. We hope they will inspire you to experiment with even more creative cookery.

APPETIZERS

BROILED GRAPEFRUIT WITH CHERRY MELOMEL

This simple appetizer is a good beginning to a light meal and a real zinger for a Sunday brunch. Or follow it with Eggs Poached in Wine (page 100) for a really special breakfast. If you're one of those folks who find wine in the morning just a hair short of immoral, remember that the heat used to broil the grapefruit evaporates the alcohol, leaving only the flavor behind.

> Grapefruit, chilled and halved
> 1 tablespoon Cherry Melomel (page 57) per grapefruit half
> 1 teaspoon light brown sugar per grapefruit half
> Maraschino cherries to garnish, halved

Section each half of a chilled grapefruit with a grapefruit knife and remove any visible seeds. Drain off excess juice and pour on a tablespoon of cherry melomel. Then sprinkle on the brown sugar and place the grapefruit under a hot broiler to brown lightly. Watch carefully, so that the sugar melts but doesn't burn. Garnish with a maraschino cherry half and serve immediately.

CHILLED SPICED SHRIMP

Few herbs stimulate the appetite as tarragon does. Combine it with shrimp and spicy, honey-laced mustard, and the interplay of subtle — and not so subtle — flavors creates a great overture to an outstanding meal.

> 10–12 fresh French tarragon leaves *or* ⅛ teaspoon dried tarragon
> ½ cup Tarragon Metheglin (page 68)
> Juice of 1 lemon
> 1 pound deveined, boiled shrimp
> Honey to taste
> ¼ cup Dijon mustard
> Lettuce
> Tarragon to garnish
> Lemon peel to garnish

Prepare a marinade by bruising a few fresh tarragon leaves and placing them in a mixing bowl large enough to hold a pound of shrimp. Add the tarragon metheglin and lemon juice. Put in the cooked, cooled shrimp and marinate for 3 to 4 hours. Make a honey-mustard dip by mixing honey into the mustard a little at a time until it reaches the desired sweetness. Start with about 1 tablespoon of honey. When you are ready to serve your appetizer, remove the shrimp from the marinade and arrange it on a lettuce-lined platter around a custard cup filled with the honey-mustard dip. Garnish with sprigs of fresh tarragon and twists of lemon peel. Serves four generously.

VEGETABLE ZINGER PIZZA

Make this vegetable pizza for any potluck, and we guarantee that all you'll bring home is the pan!

> 2 8-ounce tubes crescent rolls
> 1 8-ounce package cream cheese
> 2 tablespoons your favorite herbal metheglin (see pages 63–66)
> 1/2 cup sour cream
> 1 package Hidden Valley Ranch dressing mix, original flavor
> 1/2 head broccoli
> 1 carrot
> 2 red radishes
> 4 green onions

Preheat the oven to 350°F. Open the tubes of crescent rolls and unroll the dough without separating it into individual rolls. Arrange the dough on a cookie sheet and bake until the crust is browned on top. Allow it to cool. Soften the cream cheese by beating it with the metheglin. Add the sour cream and dressing mix and mix thoroughly. Spread the mixture on the cooled crust. Chop the broccoli, carrot, and radishes and slice the onion, including the green tops. Toss all the chopped vegetables together and spread on top of the cream-cheese mixture. In the unlikely event that you have any leftovers, this pizza keeps well in the refrigerator for several days. Just cover it with plastic wrap to keep it from drying out. Serves six to eight.

LUAU WINGS

These make great finger food for your summer luau or around-the-pool party. Kids love 'em. And they're a great warm-up for the rest of the fiesta!

> 3 pounds chicken wings, cut apart (discard the ends)
> Butter-flavored cooking spray
> 1 6-ounce can frozen orange-juice concentrate
> 2 tablespoons white country wine (see Parsley Wine, page 77)
> 1/4 cup firmly packed brown sugar
> 1 teaspoon tarragon vinegar
> 1/3 cup honey
> 1 tablespoon Dijon mustard
> Salt and pepper to taste
> 2 green onions, sliced
> Watercress and orange slices for garnish

Preheat oven to 400°F. Put chicken wings in a baking pan and spray with butter-flavored cooking spray. Bake at 400°F. for 15–20 minutes until they are tender. While the wings are baking, prepare the basting sauce as follows: Combine the orange juice, wine, brown sugar, vinegar, honey, mustard, and salt and pepper in a medium saucepan. Simmer for 4–5 minutes. Pour over the wings and reduce heat to 325°F. for 30–45 minutes, basting with sauce every 10–15 minutes. (If you'd like your wings to have a more glazed appearance, broil for a few minutes under a preheated broiler.) Sprinkle with green onions and garnish with watercress and orange slices. Serves six.

SALADS

FRUIT SALAD WITH STRAWBERRY WINE

You can vary the proportions of the fruits in this salad according to your taste, but be sure to include some of everything. Allowing the fruit mixture to sit in the refrigerator for a couple of hours before serving gives the strawberry wine time to add its delectable flavor to the individual fruits.

Cantaloupe, cut into balls or small cubes
Seedless green or red grapes, halved
Dark, sweet cherries, pitted and halved
Fresh peaches, sliced
Kiwi fruit, peeled, quartered, and sliced
Bananas, peeled and sliced
Coarsely shredded coconut
Mandarin orange slices
Strawberry Wine (page 30)
Juice of 1/2 lemon
Sugar or honey (optional)

Toss the fruits to mix them, and pour the wine liberally over the fruit. Sweeten the lemon juice with honey or sugar, if desired, and top the salad with it. Cover and refrigerate for 1–2 hours before serving. Make sure to include some of the wine-juice when you spoon this salad into fruit cups. Serves ten to twelve — more if you add extra fruit.

STRAWBERRY KIWI SALAD

This is our super-best company salad. We get more requests for this recipe than anything else we serve. It's worth the extra fooling around to make it pretty. You can serve this salad as a light lunch, with crusty French bread or thinly sliced nut bread.

Salad ingredients:
  1 pound fresh spinach
  1 bunch Cos lettuce
  1 pint strawberries
  3–4 fresh kiwi fruits
  Macadamia nuts, coarsely chopped

Wine-vinaigrette dressing:
  1/4 cup red wine vinegar (you may use strawberry or
    raspberry vinegar if desired; see Chapter 8)
  1/4 cup Strawberry Wine (page 30)
  1–2 teaspoons honey
  1 teaspoon light salad oil
  6 ripe strawberries

First, wash the spinach and lettuce in cold water and dry in a salad spinner or allow it to drain dry. (You may need to pat individual leaves dry as you assemble the salad.) Wash the berries before de-stemming, to preserve the juice, reserving six large berries for the dressing. Peel the kiwi fruit.

To assemble the salad, break the stems off the spinach leaves and arrange the leaves in a circle, tips pointing outward, on individual salad plates. Tear any remaining spinach and the lettuce leaves into bite-size pieces and put them in the center of each plate, allowing the spinach leaf tips to project for a decorative edge around the plate. Cut the strawberries into halves and slice the kiwi fruit and arrange on top of the spinach and lettuce. Sprinkle liberally with chopped macadamia nuts.

To make the dressing, put six strawberries into a blender or food processor and whirl a few times until they are chopped. Then pour in the vinegar, wine, honey, and oil and blend briefly. (You can make this dressing without the oil if you're counting calories. The small amount we add helps the dressing cling to the spinach and lettuce leaves.) Pour the wine-vinaigrette dressing over each salad and serve immediately. Makes about eight individual salads.

VEGETABLES

RED CABBAGE IN WINE

Sweet-and-sour and so pretty you'll be looking for places to serve this showy vegetable dish.

> 1 head red cabbage (about 2 pounds)
> 1 cup berry wine, except blueberry or gooseberry (see Chapter 2)
> 1/3 cup firmly packed brown sugar
> 1 teaspoon salt
> Pinch of cayenne pepper
> 4 medium apples
> 1/4 cup cider vinegar
> 1/4 cup butter

Remove the outer leaves of a head of red cabbage and discard them. Wash the cabbage in cool water and cut the head into quarters, discarding the core. Put the cabbage quarters into a large saucepan with the wine, brown sugar, salt, and cayenne pepper. Rinse, quarter, core, and peel the apples. Add the apples to the cabbage, wine, and brown sugar in the saucepan, and cover. Bring the mixture to a boil, and then reduce the heat and simmer the mixture for 20 to 30 minutes, until the apples and cabbage are tender. Remove from the heat and add the vinegar and butter. Serve immediately. Serves six to eight.

CARIBBEAN YAMS

Not your traditional candied sweet potatoes, these yummy yams are the next best thing to going on a cruise. They're delightful with a turkey dinner, heavenly with ham (especially Ham Steaks with Ginger Sauce, page 112).

> 2 medium yams
> 2 tablespoons butter
> 1/4 cup Mead (page 53)
> 1 banana, barely ripe

Peel the yams and cut into 1/2-inch slices as uniformly as possible. Melt the butter in a skillet and fry the yams until they are browned on both sides and tender. In a separate pan, sauté the banana, sliced diagonally, until it is lightly browned. Turn off the heat under the banana and add the mead, stirring to mix. Pour the banana-mead mixture over the yams and simmer gently for 2–3 minutes, turning over carefully to prevent scorching. Serves four.

GLAZED CARROTS

Just nutty enough to appeal to kids and grownups alike, these pretty glazed carrots dress up the dinner table without a lot of effort. They're great with roast chicken and present a nice textural contrast with blanched broccoli florets. Children love these — and all the alcohol will have evaporated by the time you serve them, so they can have as many as they want.

6 medium carrots
2 tablespoons butter
1 cup chicken broth or consommé
2 ounces apricot brandy
3 ounces Almond Wine (page 37)
$1/8$ teaspoon white pepper
1 teaspoon light brown sugar

Begin by peeling the carrots. Cut them into quarters lengthwise and then slice them into a saucepan in $1^{1}/_{2}$-inch lengths. Add the butter and chicken broth and cover. Cook over medium heat until the carrots are tender crisp. Remove the cover and raise the heat slightly; continue cooking until almost all the liquid is evaporated. If the carrots brown a bit, they're even tastier. Add the remaining ingredients and simmer for about 2 minutes. Serves four.

BEETS IN RED WINE SAUCE

Whether the beets you serve are Harvard or ho-hum, wait till you taste what a little red wine does for this earthy veggie.

2 tablespoons butter
1 shallot, minced
2 tablespoons flour
1-pound can beets (reserve $1/3$ cup of the beet liquid)
$1/3$ cup beef bouillon
$1/3$ cup red wine — Mulberry (page 33) or Elderberry
   (page 31)
Pinch of ground cloves (optional)

Melt the butter in a medium saucepan and stir in the minced shallot, cooking until soft, but not brown. Add the flour, stirring constantly for 1 minute. Then blend in the beet liquid, the bouillon, and the wine, stirring constantly until the sauce is smooth and thick. If desired, sprinkle the mixture lightly with ground cloves. Then add the beets and heat thoroughly. Serve immediately. Serves four.

MAIN DISHES

Eggs Poached in Wine

Any dry white wine works well with this recipe. Our favorite is Parsley Wine (page 77), but you'll find that any herbal wine or metheglin works well. Just be sure to pick a flavor you like!

> 1 tablespoon melted butter
> 1/2 cup dry white country wine
> 4 eggs
> Salt and pepper to taste
> 2 tablespoons Roquefort cheese, crumbled
> Buttered toast rounds

In a skillet, combine the butter and the wine. Heat the mixture until it's quite hot, but not boiling. Then carefully slip the eggs into the liquid one at a time, being careful not to break the yolks. Season with salt and pepper and cook gently until the whites are almost set. Then sprinkle on the cheese. Continue cooking until the eggs are done to your taste and the cheese has melted. Serve on buttered toast rounds. Serves two to four.

Sirloin Strips with Wine Sauce

Serve these steaks with potatoes that have been cut into wedges, parboiled, and then crisped in a little hot oil.

> 4 sirloin strips, about 3/4 inch thick
> 1 tablespoon cornstarch
> 2 cloves garlic, minced
> 1 tablespoon butter
> 1/4 cup finely sliced green onion
> 1/4 cup beef broth
> 1/4 cup Sweet Port-Style Blackberry Wine (page 20)
> Salt and pepper
> 2 tablespoons butter
> Parsley to garnish

Rub steaks on both sides with cornstarch and sprinkle with minced garlic. Heat a tablespoon of butter in a heavy skillet and brown the steaks on both sides. Then reduce the heat and sauté the steaks to the desired degree of doneness — about 4 minutes on each side for rare, up to 9 or 10 minutes for well done. Remove steaks to a warm platter. Make the wine sauce by adding green onion to the pan and sautéing for a few minutes until soft but not browned. Add the beef broth and wine and heat just to the boiling point. Add salt and pepper to taste. Then whisk in the 2 tablespoons of butter a little at a time until the sauce is smooth. You can mix a little water with a teaspoon of cornstarch to make a roux and add it to the sauce to make it smoother. Pour the sauce over the steaks, sprinkle with a little extra onion, and garnish with parsley. Serves four.

CHICKEN BREASTS DIANE WITH PARSLEY WINE

For a light and healthy meal, serve this low-cholesterol dish with steamed broccoli, a fresh, green salad, and crusty French bread.

> 4 large boneless split chicken breasts
> 1/2 teaspoon salt
> 1/4–1/2 teaspoon black pepper
> Butter-flavored cooking spray
> 4 tablespoons olive oil
> 3 tablespoons chopped fresh chives or green onions
> Juice of 1/2 lemon
> 2 tablespoons Parsley Wine (page 77) or Parsley
>   Metheglin (see pages 63–66)
> 3 tablespoons chopped parsley
> 2 teaspoons Dijon mustard
> 1/4 cup chicken broth

Put the chicken breasts between two sheets of waxed paper or plastic wrap and pound slightly with a mallet to make sure that the breasts are of an even thickness. Then sprinkle with salt and pepper. Spray a skillet with a generous amount of butter-flavored cooking spray and add 1–2 tablespoons of olive oil. Heat the oil and then add the chicken. Cook the chicken over high heat for about 3 minutes. Do not overcook, or the breasts will be dry. Transfer the chicken to a warm serving platter. Add chives or green onions, lemon juice, wine, chopped parsley, and mustard to the pan and cook for about 15 seconds, whisking constantly. Now whisk in the broth and stir until the sauce is smooth. Whisk in the remaining olive oil. Pour the sauce over the chicken and serve immediately. Serves four.

ROAST LEG OF LAMB WITH SPICY WINE SAUCE

No shy little lamb, this! If you've always thought that lamb meant monotonous, wait till you see what this zippy sauce does for a laid-back leg of lamb.

>1 cup Sweet Port-Style Blackberry Wine (page 20)
>1/4 cup salad oil
>1 onion, coarsely chopped
>2 cloves garlic, minced
>2 teaspoons salt
>1/2 teaspoon Tabasco
>1 whole leg of lamb (6–8 pounds)
>Parsley and mint to garnish

Make a marinade by combining the wine, salad oil, onion, garlic, salt, and Tabasco. Marinate the lamb for 8 hours or overnight, turning occasionally. Place the marinated lamb on a rack in a shallow roasting pan and roast at 325°F. for 25 minutes for each pound of lamb. When the roast is browned and done to taste, remove it to a platter decorated with parsley and sprigs of mint and serve. Serves twelve to sixteen.

BRATWURST IN DILL METHEGLIN

If ever a recipe were invented to demonstrate how wines can turn everyday fare into a celebration, this is it. Even the lowly bratwurst makes a gourmet meal when you cook it in a delightful dill metheglin. Your guests may decide that potluck at your place is preferable to party fare somewhere else! Serve with dill pickles, onions, and a good-quality mustard. These are great with corn chips that have been crisped in the oven and your favorite dip, or with baked beans or potato salad.

8–10 bratwurst
1 25-ounce bottle Dill Metheglin (see pages 63–66)
1 jar sauerkraut to taste
Dill seed to taste
1 package hot dog buns, warmed

Put the bratwurst into a saucepan and add enough dill metheglin to cover. Simmer for 6–8 minutes until they are plumped and heated through. Then add the sauerkraut and dill seed as desired to the broth and cook until hot. Drain the sauerkraut. Put the brats on freshly warmed buns lined with kraut. Serves eight to ten.

COUNTRY-STYLE BEEF BURGUNDY

Simple as stew, but twice as savory, this hearty dish is sure to please the beef lovers at your family table. Serve over rice or noodles with French bread or hard rolls and a green salad.

2 slices bacon
2 pounds beef round tip steak, cut into 2-inch cubes
2 tablespoons flour
1 teaspoon seasoned salt
1 package beef stew seasoning mix
1 cup Sweet Port-Style Blackberry Wine (page 20)
1 cup water
1 tablespoon tomato paste
12 small boiling onions
4 ounces sautéed mushrooms
16 cherry tomatoes

Fry the bacon and remove it from the skillet, reserving the drippings. Dredge the beef cubes in flour and seasoned salt and fry in bacon drippings. When the meat is browned on all sides, add the seasoning mix, wine, water, and tomato paste. Cover and simmer for 45 minutes. Then peel the onions, piercing the ends with a fork so they retain their shape, add them to the pan, and simmer for 40 minutes more. Add the mushrooms and cherry tomatoes and simmer for 3 additional minutes. Serves four to six.

Roast Pork Loin with Peach Sauce

Since we usually finish this roast on the grill, it's one of our favorite dishes for outdoor entertainment. We like it with a fresh fruit salad and broasted new potatoes, cooked with julienned peppers and sliced onions in foil packets on the grill.

1 25-ounce bottle Peach Wine (page 26)
1 teaspoon ginger, minced
3–4 dashes of bottled teriyaki sauce *or* 1/4 cup bottled
    teriyaki glaze
1/4 cup peanut oil (or other light oil)
1 4-pound pork loin roast or backstrap
1 cup sugar
1 cup water
1 teaspoon cornstarch
2 cups freshly sliced peaches
1 cup peach brandy
Fresh mint for garnish

Mix 1 cup of the peach wine, the ginger, the teriyaki sauce, and the peanut oil. Use this mixture to marinate the pork loin for 12 hours or overnight, rolling the roast in the marinade two or three times during the marinating process. Then place the marinated roast in a covered Dutch oven with the remaining peach wine and roast at 350°F. for 1 to 1 1/2 hours, depending on the size of the roast. At this point, we usually move the roast to the grill and smoke it with mesquite chips for about half an hour or until it is brown on the outside. But it is also good if you simply remove the cover from the Dutch oven and roast it for an additional half hour or until it is browned on the outside. Then remove the roast and use the pan and the drippings to make the sauce. Just mix the sugar and water with the drippings and heat. Then dissolve the cornstarch in a little water and add, stirring with a whisk until the mixture begins to thicken. Add the fresh peaches and the peach brandy. Once the sauce thickens, remove it from the heat, slice the roast pork, and pour or ladle the sauce over the meat. Garnish with a sprig or two of fresh mint. Serves six to eight.

PEACHY BARBECUE RIBS

Try these tasty ribs with baked beans and cole slaw or potato salad.

>   4 meaty spare ribs (about 2½ pounds)
>   1 onion, sliced
>   2 cups Peach Wine (page 26)
>   1 12-ounce bottle beer
>   1 15-ounce can tomato sauce
>   1 clove garlic, minced
>   1 cup unsweetened pineapple juice
>   ½ teaspoon salt
>   ⅓ cup brown sugar
>   ½ teaspoon Liquid Smoke
>   2 tablespoons red wine vinegar
>   Dash of hot pepper sauce

Trim any excess fat from the ribs and place them in a deep saucepan or Dutch oven with the sliced onion, the peach wine, and the beer. Marinate for 1–2 hours, then put the pan on the stove top and simmer the ribs for 1–2 hours, depending on their meatiness. When the ribs are tender, remove them from the pan and put them on the grill with charcoal and mesquite chips for flavor. Meanwhile, combine the tomato sauce, garlic, pineapple juice, salt, brown sugar, Liquid Smoke, red wine vinegar, and hot pepper sauce in a saucepan and bring to a boil. Allow the mixture to simmer until the ribs start to brown; then ladle the sauce onto the ribs and continue to barbecue them slowly, turning the ribs several times and basting with sauce at each turn. They're done when the sauce has formed a glaze on the ribs — usually 10–15 minutes on a slow grill, but this varies considerably according to the heat of the coals and the distance of the meat from the coals. Serves four.

RICH'S HOLIDAY TURKEY

Several of our friends told us that they'd buy this book just for the Holiday Turkey recipe. Some were even sacrilegious enough to say they'd send it to their mothers.

So far as we can tell, the only problem you'll run into with this roast turkey is that you can't count on leftovers — there won't be any! And the turkey won't be the only thing to disappear in record time. Once your family and friends discover what tangerine melomel does to the gravy — and what sage metheglin does to stuffing — Thanksgiving at your house may become a family tradition. And so will your country wines.

You'll need a large hypodermic needle — the kind that veterinarians use, with a large needle and a barrel that holds about 60 cc's — to inject the turkey with the Tangerine Melomel — the secret ingredient! These needles are inexpensive and easy to obtain — just ask your pharmacist.

> 1 roasting turkey, 12–15 pounds, completely thawed
> 1 1/2–2 25-ounce bottles Tangerine Melomel (page 61)

Ingredients for stuffing:
> 2 tablespoons butter
> 1/2 cup diced celery
> 1 small red onion, chopped
> 1 small white onion, chopped
> 1 small clove garlic, minced
> 1/2 cup chicken stock
> Sage to taste
> 1/8 teaspoon each: tarragon, basil, oregano, and coarsely
>   ground black pepper
> 1/2 cup Sage Metheglin (see pages 63–66)
> 4–6 cups dry French bread, broken into small pieces

Optional:
> Add any of the following items. Our favorite with this
> turkey is sliced mandarin oranges, but you may also add
> 1/2–1 cup of *cooked* sausage, or oysters, walnuts, or
> apples.

Begin by rinsing the turkey inside and out and drying it with a cloth. Then rub the cavity with a little salt and set the turkey aside in the roasting pan you'll use for baking. Prepare the stuffing by melting the butter in a saucepan and adding the celery, red and white onions, and garlic, cooking slowly just until tender. Add the chicken stock and turn off the heat. Add herbs, spices, and any optional items, such as the mandarin orange slices or walnuts. Add the sage metheglin and pour the mixture over the bread pieces in a large mixing bowl. Toss to distribute the moisture evenly, but use a light touch — the bread pieces should stay separate. Now stuff the bird — and don't forget the neck cavity. Most turkeys come with a metal cleat to tuck the legs under, but if yours doesn't, truss and tie the legs down.

When the turkey is stuffed and ready for the oven, use a hypodermic needle to inject the turkey with several "shots" of tangerine melomel. Retain the rest of the melomel for basting, and baste frequently as the turkey roasts to keep it moist and flavorful. To determine doneness, you may use a meat thermometer or test by moving a leg back and forth. If the leg moves easily in the joint, the bird is done. When the turkey is done, remove it to a platter and allow it to sit for a few minutes to make slicing easier.

In the meantime, skim off and discard any excess fat from the pan juices and add water or broth to the pan, if necessary, to make the number of cups of gravy you'll need. Bring the mixture to a boil and add cornstarch mixed into a cup of water to thicken. (The amount of cornstarch and water you add will depend on how much gravy you're making.) Stir continuously with a wire whisk to prevent lumps as the gravy thickens. For a traditional holiday meal, serve your turkey and dressing with mashed potatoes, cranberry sauce, and the vegetables, salads, and desserts that make the holidays special at your house. Serves ten to twelve.

DILLY WINE AND CHEESE VEGGIE CASSEROLE

This is a family favorite because it has more flavor for less work than almost anything else we make, yet the addition of a little wine makes it unusual enough that someone is always asking for the recipe.

   1/2 pound American cheese
   1/4 cup Dill Metheglin (see pages 63–66)
   1/2 cup butter
   1 16-ounce bag frozen mixed vegetables containing
      broccoli, cauliflower, and carrots, thawed
   1 tablespoon chopped fresh dill *or* 1 teaspoon dried dill
   1 cup (about 30) crushed butter crackers

Cut the cheese into cubes and melt it in a saucepan with the wine and half of the butter, stirring often until it is smooth. Place the vegetables in a 1-quart casserole and pour the cheese mixture over them, mixing well. Melt the remaining butter and stir in the cracker crumbs. Sprinkle over the top of the casserole and bake, uncovered, at 350°F. for 20–25 minutes, or until the crumb topping is lightly browned. Serve at once with crusty French bread and a green salad. Serves four to six.

SCALLOPINE ALMANDINE

This dish is a natural with a variety of cheesey pasta dishes. We particularly like it with linguini sauced with a blend of cheeses and cream as follows: Sauté 1/4 cup minced onion and 1 clove of minced garlic in 2 tablespoons of butter. When both are clear but not browned, add a 6-ounce package of cream cheese, 1/2 cup of grated Parmesan cheese, 1/8 cup of dried parsley, and 1 1/2 cups of light cream, and simmer just until the sauce is smooth. You can add 1/4 cup of almond wine for a nuttier taste. The veal is equally good with spaghetti or other pasta side dishes.

1/2 cup flour
1/4 teaspoon garlic powder
1/4 teaspoon salt
1/8 teaspoon black pepper
1 1/2 pounds veal scallops
3 tablespoons butter or oil
2 tablespoons chopped shallots
1/2 pound mushrooms, sliced
2 tablespoons brandy
3 tablespoons Almond Wine (page 37)
1 tablespoon butter

Prepare a seasoned mixture for dredging the veal scallops, using the flour, garlic powder, salt, and pepper. Pound the scallops to an even thickness and dredge them in the flour mixture until they are evenly coated. Then sauté the scallops in 3 tablespoons butter or oil over medium high heat just until both sides are golden brown. Remove the meat to a platter and keep it warm while you sauté the shallots and mushrooms in the same butter or oil (add a little more if needed).

Cook for 4–5 minutes or until the mushrooms are tender. Then return the meat to the pan and cook for 2–3 minutes more, turning as needed.

Remove the meat to a warmed platter and deglaze the pan with the brandy and the wine, adding 1 tablespoon more butter. Pour the sauce over the scallops and serve immediately. Serves four to six.

COUNTRY-STYLE CORNISH HEN DU BOIS WITH BLACKBERRY SAUCE

4 Cornish hens
Salt and pepper to taste
1 medium onion, peeled and quartered
1 apple, quartered (leave the peel on)
2–3 outside stalks of celery
2 cups water

Sauce:
1 cup drippings and broth from the roasting pan
1–2 cloves garlic, minced (or to taste)
1/2 crushed bay leaf (mid-rib removed)
1 cup chicken stock or bouillon
3 ounces Sweet Port-Style Blackberry Wine (page 20)
1 heaping tablespoon cornstarch
2 tablespoons cold water
2 cups blackberries, fresh or frozen
Salt and pepper to taste
1 tablespoon lemon juice
Pinch of sugar

Preheat the oven to 325°F. Rinse the Cornish hens and dry with a kitchen towel. Rub salt and pepper on both the inside and the outside. Stuff each hen with 1/4 onion, 1/4 apple, and some celery, broken to fit. (You will ultimately discard the stuffing items.) Roast the hens on a rack in a roasting pan with 2 cups of water until they are tender and do not bleed when you stick a fork into them; check after 45 minutes. During the first part of the roasting period, tent the hens with foil to keep them from browning too fast. For the last 10 minutes of cooking time, remove the tent and turn the oven up to 400°F. so that the hens brown evenly. When they are done, remove the stuffing and discard. Cut the hens in half with scissors, splitting the breasts and leaving wings and legs attached. Arrange the halves on a platter and keep them warm while you make the sauce.

Draw the pan drippings off with a baster or syringe and pour them into a skillet. Add the garlic, bay leaf, chicken stock, and blackberry wine. Simmer for 3–4 minutes and strain into a 1-quart saucepan. Dissolve the cornstarch in 2 tablespoons of cold water and stir into the sauce. Add the blackberries and simmer for 3 more minutes. Season to taste with salt, pepper, lemon juice, and a pinch of sugar. Pour over the hens and serve at once. Serves four.

COUNTRY-STYLE DUCK FLAMBÉ WITH APRICOTS

Okay, you don't have to set it on fire. But if you've never tried a flambé dish, this is an easy way to start. Your guests will surely be impressed, and the flame helps evaporate the alcohol in the brandy so you don't have "drunken duck."

> 1 duck, about 4 pounds
> Salt and pepper to taste
> 2 or 3 unpeeled apples, quartered
> 2 cups water
> 1/4 cup slivered almonds
> 1 tablespoon butter
> 1/4 cup Tangerine Melomel (page 61)
> 1/4 cup Almond Wine (page 37)
> 1 15-ounce can apricots
> 2 tablespoons brown sugar
> 1/8 teaspoon garlic powder
> 1 teaspoon soy sauce
> 3 ounces apricot brandy
> Parsley to garnish

Preheat oven to 325°F. Rinse and dry the duck and remove the first two sections of wings. Rub the duck inside and out with salt and pepper and stuff with the apples. Then place it on a raised rack in a roasting pan with 2 cups of water to keep it moist during roasting. Put a heavy foil tent over the duck for most of the roasting time so it doesn't brown too quickly. Make a basting sauce by browning the almonds in butter. Then add the tangerine melomel, the almond wine, and the juice from the canned apricots. Dissolve the brown sugar in the basting sauce and add the garlic powder and soy sauce. For the last 10 minutes of roasting time, remove the tent, raise the oven temperature to 400°F., and baste the duck several times. When the duck is browned and crisp, remove it from the roasting pan and place it and the apricots on an ovenproof platter in a 200°F. oven. Deglaze the pan drippings with apricot brandy to make a flambé sauce. When the apricots are heated through, pour the hot flambé sauce over the duck and tuck some parsley sprigs in among the apricots. For a really impressive entrée, light the sauce while it's hot and serve immediately. Serves four to six.

SWEET-AND-SOUR SHRIMP

If you're one of those folks who always thinks there's too much ginger in Oriental cooking, you may find that this sweet-and-sour shrimp is just the ticket. The ginger metheglin is a bit mellower and more subtle than pure ginger.

    ¹/₄ cup brown sugar
    2 tablespoons cornstarch
    ¹/₂ teaspoon salt
    ¹/₄ cup vinegar
    1 tablespoon soy sauce
    ¹/₄ cup Ginger Metheglin (page 66)
    1 large (#2) can pineapple chunks and syrup
    1 green pepper, diced
    2 small onions, cut into rings
    1 pound shrimp, deveined and cooked
    3 cups cooked rice

In a saucepan combine the brown sugar, cornstarch, and salt; mix until smooth. Add the vinegar, soy sauce, ginger metheglin, and syrup drained from the pineapple. Simmer, stirring constantly, until the mixture is slightly thickened. In another pan, sauté green pepper, onion, and pineapple chunks until the onion is tender. Then add to the sauce and simmer for 2 minutes. Add the shrimp and bring to a boil, stirring constantly. Serve over hot rice. Serves four to six.

Ham Steaks with Ginger Sauce

¹/₂ cup water
2 tablespoons brown sugar
¹/₄ teaspoon salt
¹/₄ cup Ginger Metheglin (page 66)
1 tablespoon cornstarch
2 tablespoons cold water
4 pineapple rings
1 tablespoon butter
4 ham steaks, about ³/₄ inch thick

Preheat the oven to 350°F. While the oven is heating, make the ginger sauce. Combine ¹/₂ cup water in a saucepan with the brown sugar and salt and bring to a boil. Add the ginger metheglin and simmer until the sugar is dissolved. Mix the cornstarch with 2 tablespoons cold water and whisk into the sauce, stirring constantly until the sauce is clear and thickened (about 3 minutes). Keep the sauce warm while you prepare the pineapple. Drain the pineapple rings and pat dry with a paper towel. Melt the butter in a skillet and brown the pineapple rings. Arrange the ham steaks in a baking dish and top each one with a pineapple ring. Pour the sauce over the ham and pineapple and bake for about 25 minutes, basting several times with the sauce. When the ham is done, serve it with candied yams for a down-South supper. Serves four.

Orange Roughy with Macadamia Sauce

Butter-flavored cooking spray
3–4 sprigs parsley
1 3¹/₂-ounce jar macadamia nuts
4 orange roughy filets
Juice of 1 lemon
2 tablespoons butter
1 tablespoon flour
¹/₄ cup honey wine (see Chapter 4)
³/₄ cup light cream
Parsley to garnish

Preheat oven to 350°F. Spray the inside of a baking pan with butter-flavored cooking spray. Chop the parsley fine. Chop the macadamia nuts and mix about a third of them with the chopped parsley. Spray both sides of the roughy with cooking spray and then roll it in the parsley-macadamia mixture. Arrange the filets in the baking pan and squeeze the lemon juice over them. Bake until the roughy is flaky when you pull it apart with a fork. Do not overcook. While the roughy is baking, make a sauce by sautéing the rest of the chopped macadamia nuts in the butter briefly and adding the flour. Continue to cook until the flour is slightly browned. Now add the honey wine and bring to a boil, stirring continuously with a wire whisk. Add the cream and continue to whisk until the mixture thickens slightly. Remove from the heat and ladle onto warm plates. Put a roughy filet on top of the sauce on each plate and garnish with parsley sprigs. Serves four.

SAUCY SHRIMP CREOLE

You can enjoy this dish as it is or turn it into a gumbo by adding ¹/₂ cup of chopped ham and 1 cup of sliced okra and thickening the sauce just a bit. Substantial and savory, it's delicious served with hot rice, generously laced with chopped parsley.

> 1¹/₂ cups chopped onion
> 1 cup chopped celery
> 1 medium green pepper, chopped fine
> 2 cloves garlic, minced
> ¹/₄ cup butter
> 1 15-ounce can tomato sauce
> ¹/₂ cup water
> ¹/₂ cup Parsley Wine (page 77)
> 1¹/₂ teaspoons salt
> ¹/₈ teaspoon cayenne
> 2 bay leaves
> 2 teaspoons chopped parsley
> 14–16 ounces fresh, cleaned shrimp
> 3 cups hot, cooked rice

Sauté onion, celery, green pepper, and garlic in butter until onion is tender. Remove from heat and stir in tomato sauce, water, parsley wine, and seasonings. Simmer uncovered for 10 minutes, adding water if needed. Stir in the shrimp and heat to boiling; cover and simmer over medium heat 10–20 minutes or until shrimp are pink and tender. Remove the bay leaves. Serve over rice. Serves four to six.

MARINADES

MARINADE ORIENTAL

This marinade is excellent for beef, chicken, or pork to be used in Oriental cooking.

> $^1/_2$ cup red wine vinegar
> $^1/_2$ cup Ginger Metheglin (page 66)
> $^1/_4$ cup soy sauce
> 1 tablespoon sesame oil
> 1 tablespoon brown sugar
> $^1/_4$ teaspoon minced garlic

Mix all the ingredients.

HERBAL MARINADE

This marinade really adds sparkle to chicken, pork, and veal dishes.

> $^1/_2$ cup white vinegar
> $^1/_2$ cup Lemon-Thyme Metheglin (page 69)
> 2 tablespoons olive oil
> $^1/_4$ teaspoon sweet basil (dried)
> $^1/_4$ teaspoon garlic, minced
> $^1/_2$ minced onion
> $^1/_8$ teaspoon oregano (dried)
> $^1/_8$ teaspoon tarragon (dried)
> 2 tablespoons lemon juice

Mix all the ingredients.

SPICY MARINADE

This marinade works especially well with chicken and pork that will be used in Mexican cooking. We like it best with cubed chicken that is to be grilled with mushrooms, cherry tomatoes, and chunks of green peppers on a skewer and served with warm flour tortillas.

  $^1/_2$ cup Sweet Port-Style Blackberry Wine (page 20)
  2 tablespoons olive oil
  3 tablespoons hot pepper sauce
  1 clove garlic, minced
  $^1/_4$ teaspoon chili powder
  $^1/_8$ teaspoon salt
  $^1/_8$ teaspoon black pepper
  1 tablespoon chopped coriander or parsley

Mix all the ingredients.

DESSERTS

ZABAGLIONE (WINE CUSTARD)

Mild wines like Peach Wine (page 26) are nice in this recipe, as are berry wines (Chapter 2).

  6 egg yolks
  $^1/_2$ cup sugar
  $^1/_8$ teaspoon salt
  1 cup country wine

Beat the egg yolks with the sugar and salt until the mixture is thick and lemon colored. Stir in the wine and cook in a double boiler over simmering water, beating constantly with a rotary beater until the mixture foams and thickens. It will double or triple in volume. Turn the custard into sherbet glasses and chill at least an hour, or until serving time. Serves eight to ten.

Peachy Bread Pudding

6 egg yolks
²/₃ cup sugar
Dash of salt
1¹/₂ cups Peach Wine (page 26)
1¹/₂ cups half-and-half
¹/₂ teaspoon vanilla
3–4 cups dried French bread, broken into small pieces
²/₃ cup chopped pecans
Heavy cream

Beat the egg yolks with the sugar and salt in a mixing bowl until the mixture is thick and lemon colored. Add the wine and place the mixture in the top of a double boiler over simmering water, beating it constantly with a hand mixer or rotary beater. When the custard is thick and foamy — it will look a little like pale yellow meringue and will hold peaks when you lift the beater — gently fold in the half-and-half and the vanilla and pour the custard over the bread pieces. Stir in the chopped pecans and bake the mixture in a slow oven (325°F.) until a knife inserted into the center of the pudding comes out clean; start checking at about 30 minutes. Serve warm with fresh cream or chill and garnish with a little whipped cream. Serves six to eight.

Drunken Apricots

6 canned whole apricots, pitted
6 ounces Southern Comfort
1 25-ounce bottle Tangerine Melomel (page 61)
1 pint half-and-half or light cream

Chill all the ingredients until they are very cold. Skewer a whole apricot on a long wooden skewer or drink stirrer and place it in the bottom of a tulip-shaped champagne glass. Place the glasses with the apricots in the freezer until apricots are firm. When you are ready to serve, pour each of the following ingredients gently into the glass, starting with 1 ounce of Southern Comfort, adding enough tangerine melomel to nearly fill the glass, and finishing with an ounce of half-and-half. Serves six.

BRANDIED CHERRIES WITH CHERRY MELOMEL

This is a pretty and easy-to-assemble dessert if you make the pudding a day in advance. Canned or "instant" puddings will do in a pinch, but the homemade variety makes this dessert extra special.

2 cups whole milk
1/4 cup cornstarch
2/3 cup sugar
1/4 teaspoon salt
3 egg yolks
2 tablespoons butter
1/2 teaspoon vanilla
1 16-ounce can cherry pie filling
1/3 cup Cherry Melomel (page 57)
2 tablespoons brandy
1 teaspoon vanilla
Whipped cream and slivered almonds for garnish

Scald the milk in a saucepan or microwave oven and cool slightly. Mix the cornstarch, sugar, and salt and gradually add the milk. Cook over moderate heat, stirring constantly, until the mixture thickens and boils. Continue to boil, still stirring constantly, for 2 minutes, and then remove from the heat. Beat the egg yolks and add a small amount of the pudding to them. Mix thoroughly and add the egg-yolk mixture to the rest of the pudding. Cook 1 minute more, stirring constantly. Add the butter and vanilla and stir. Allow the pudding to cool.

Now mix the cherry pie filling, cherry melomel, brandy, and vanilla. Distribute half the cherry mixture equally among eight wine goblets. On top of each, spoon some of the cooled vanilla pudding. Then add the rest of the brandied cherries, reserving eight cherries for a garnish. Chill and serve. Top the goblets with a dollop of whipped cream and a few slivered almonds, if desired. Serves ten to twelve.

PEAR TULIPS

This is just about the easiest dessert we can think of. The presentation is unique and the tangerine melomel adds just the right touch.

1 large (2-pound) can pears
1 cup whipping cream
1 cup sour cream
$^1/_4$ cup Tangerine Melomel (page 61)
Grated unsweetened chocolate for garnish
Slivered almonds for garnish

Remove the pears from the can carefully so you don't break them. Join two halves together to form one whole pear and place the narrow ends down in a tulip-shaped champagne glass. Chill while you whip 1 cup of cream. Fold the whipped cream into the sour cream and then fold in the tangerine melomel. Spoon this mixture over the pears and sprinkle with grated unsweetened chocolate and slivered almonds. Serves four to six.

HEAVENLY HAZELNUT PIE

If there's anything we love it's a dessert that ought to make you feel guilty, but doesn't. This one's low on fat — but it tastes so good you'll probably offset the calorie advantage by having seconds. To toast the hazelnuts and the coconut, spread them on a cookie sheet and place it in a 350°F. oven. Stir frequently for about 10 minutes until the coconut is golden.

1 package macaroons
$1^1/_2$ ounces Hazelnut Wine (page 36)
1 pint white chocolate frozen yogurt
$^1/_2$ cup hazelnuts, toasted
2 tablespoons coconut, toasted

Dry the macaroons overnight or place them in an oven that's been heated to 250°F. and then turned off, for about 45 minutes. Then crush them and soak them in the hazelnut wine. Butter a 9-inch pie tin or glass pan and press the crumbs into it to make a crust. Beat the frozen yogurt until it's slightly softened and blend in three-quarters of the toasted hazelnuts. Spoon the frozen yogurt into the pie dish, mounding it slightly in the center. Sprinkle with the remaining toasted hazelnuts and the toasted coconut. Freeze for 2–3 hours before serving. Serves eight.

For the crust:
   1½ cups crushed chocolate wafers
   ⅓ cup butter
   ½ tablespoon sugar

For the filling:
   2 1-ounce squares sweet chocolate
   2 8-ounce packages cream cheese
   4 eggs
   ¾ cup sugar
   2–3 teaspoons instant coffee
   3 tablespoons Sweet Red Raspberry Wine (page 28)
   Dash of salt
   Chocolate shavings for garnish
   Fresh raspberries for garnish

Preheat the oven to 350°F. Crush the wafers and combine the wafer crumbs, butter, and ½ tablespoon of sugar. Press onto the sides and bottom of a buttered 8-inch spring-form pan. Then melt the chocolate over hot, but not boiling, water and stir until smooth. In the small bowl of an electric mixer, beat the cream cheese until it's soft and smooth. Then add the eggs, one at a time, to the cream cheese. When the eggs are fully blended, add ¾ cup of sugar gradually, mixing until well blended. Add the melted chocolate, the instant coffee, the raspberry wine, and the salt, stirring until well blended. Turn the mixture into the prepared pan and bake for about 40 minutes or until the cake center is almost set. Wiggle the pan back and forth, and remove from the oven when the part that ripples in the center of the pan is about the size of a half dollar. Or insert a knife halfway between the edge and the center of the pan; when it comes out clean, the cheesecake is finished. It will get firmer when chilled. Cool on the countertop for about an hour and then cover and chill for at least 4 hours or overnight. Remove the sides of the pan and garnish the cheesecake with chocolate shavings and fresh raspberries. Serves eight.

8

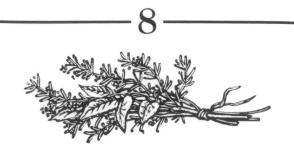

Making Vinegars from Country Wines

The natural result of the winemaking process, if we didn't interrupt it with such devices as airlocked fermentation vessels and tightly corked bottles, would be vinegar. If you've always thought of vinegar in terms of the distilled variety you buy at the market or the more flavorful cider vinegar that sits next to it on the shelf, a whole world of subtle and intriguing flavors awaits you when you start making vinegars from your own homemade wines. As salads claim an ever-increasing place in health- and weight-conscious Americans' diets, the demand for wine and herbal vinegars is also increasing.

Most wine vinegars available in gourmet shops come from a limited number of red and white grape wines. Vinegars from finer wines are rare — and expensive. You wouldn't fare very well if you tried to make your own wine vinegars from inexpensive jug wines, either. Commercial wines, except for the expensive vintage varieties no one would want to turn into vinegar, are often pasteurized or treated with chemical preservatives to make shipping and storage easier by keeping the wine from turning into vinegar!

Since few homemade wines have preservatives added, it's easy to turn them into delectable and deliciously different salad and pickling vinegars. You'll need little equipment, and the process itself is simple, requiring only a couple of minutes a day. But before we look at the methods you'll use to begin making vinegar, we do need to give you a word of warning: *Don't make vinegar in the cellar where you store your wine*. The presence of vinegar may cause your wine to turn. And although any vinegars you make from homemade wines will likely be the best you've ever tasted, you'd hardly want gallons and gallons of the stuff. A little vinegar, after all, goes a long way.

In our winemaking experience we have found a few experimental wine varieties that didn't quite suit our tastes — maybe the herb flavor of a metheglin was a little too strong, or we thought a blend of herbs and spices overpowered the subtle honey taste we sought to enhance. Sometimes the problem can be solved by blending wines. (Commercial bottlers are often prohibited by law from blending vintages, but some of our favorites evolved from blending. Home winemakers are free to experiment in any way they like.) But occasionally a wine seems better suited to a salad than a wineglass. That's when we make wine vinegar.

THE VINEGAR CASK

Although it is possible to use glass or plastic containers when you're making vinegar, wood is far superior. Being inert, glass and plastic containers can actually inhibit the vinegar-making process because they don't "breathe" as wood does. And bacteria that cause the chemical reaction resulting in vinegar need oxygen to grow as surely as wine yeast needs an absence of oxygen to produce sufficient alcohol. Wooden containers may also help ensure that the bacteria, *acetobacter*, remain healthy and growing as new wine is added to the vat, tub, or keg. Being organic and capable of absorbing a little vinegar, wood helps hold some of these bacteria even as vinegar is drained off and new wine is added.

If you really get into vinegar making, you'll tap your vinegar cask frequently, bottle the results with a sprig of fresh herb in each bottle, and earn a reputation as an exceptionally creative gift-giver. Once you hear the rave reviews from folks who've tried your homemade wine vinegars, you'll agree the time and trouble you took to find a wooden container was well spent. As you use it over and over, adding new wine to the top as you remove vinegar from the spigot at the bottom, you'll find each batch of vinegar has its own subtle personality. If you create the ultimate vinegar, you may want to reserve a second container just for that variety.

Almost any small wooden container — a tub or a small keg, a wooden planter for which you've made a plywood top — will suit your needs. One of our favorite vinegar containers is an old wooden butter churn with the dasher missing. It has a wooden top with a hole in it, and we added a spigot near the bottom to draw off the vinegar. Spigots are available from a number of mail-order sources, and you need only drill a hole in the container and affix one. The ideal vinegar-making vessel is a fairly small wooden cask or barrel (from 1 to 3 gallons) with a bung hole at the top and a spigot on one end, a few inches from the bottom. The spigot is always necessary because the usable vinegar must be extracted from the *lower* portion of the container, where the strongest vinegar will sink during the fermentation process.

The first thing to do, once you've found or purchased your container, is to scrub it clean with soap and water. Rinse again and still again and let it dry thoroughly.

A small wooden barrel with a bung hole on the top and a spigot on the end makes an ideal vinegar cask.

We like to get the process started by making use of the leftovers from winemaking, but you can also begin by using a good-quality wine vinegar to act as a starter and proceed from there. We'll show you how to use both methods. Whichever way you choose, you're sure to be delighted with the results.

USING LEFTOVER MUST

In winemaking countries, the leftover must is sometimes made into *vinello*, a weaker wine with a lower alcohol content, by adding about a third the amount of water that was added to the original wine recipe and letting the mixture ferment again for about a week. Since this "small" wine has only 6 to 8 percent alcohol, it keeps well for only about 2 months. The flavor is also weaker than that of the original recipe. Serving a guest the "smalls" sometimes indicates that the host regards him as not quite important enough to be served the "real thing."

But the leftover must does contain the ingredients necessary to make a fine vinegar, because vinegar can be made from any liquid capable of being converted into alcohol. Your leftover must will contain some residual sugars, which in the presence of oxygen and *acetobacter* will form acetic acid and water (what we commonly call vinegar). It will also contain some organic acids and esters derived from the fruit, and that's where the flavor comes from.

If you make your starter from the fermented solids left over from winemaking, the process has the virtue of using what you might otherwise throw away or add to the compost heap (to the delight of the earthworms!). Once you've syphoned off a wine for its second fermentation, put the leftover solids into the bottom of a glass or plastic container or a wooden bowl and let it sit in the open air for 2 or 3 days, uncovered.

You'll know you're ready for the next step in the process when you begin to smell vinegar. Pour some lukewarm water over the mixture and strain the liquid into your keg. Fill it to about a tenth of its capacity. Then every day for the next 8 to 10 days, add about the same amount of lukewarm water until you've filled the keg.

(You can also add any complementary wine that may be available at this time — partial bottles remaining after serving, wine that's left when you're bottling and have too little excess to fill another bottle, or the product of experiments that didn't quite meet your expectations.) If your container is quite large, you may need to add a little wine to make sure your solution doesn't become too dilute. If we're making more than a gallon of vinegar by this method, we always add at least 1–2 pints of wine to the container.

By the time the keg is full, the *mother* (a thick film of *acetobacter*) will have started to form on the top of your vinegar. Years ago, we called this "the old lady" when it formed in the vinegar bottle. Whatever you call it, it's necessary to the vinegar-making process.

The next step is to open the spigot and extract the liquid a little at a time over the next month — about a cupful every day or two. Pour the liquid taken from the bottom of the container back in through the bung hole. Use a funnel and insert a tube of some kind into the keg (we use plastic aquarium tubing or a plastic drinking straw), so that you make an opening in the mother. The liquid you're adding is the weakest part of the solution and needs to get close to the mother to be made stronger. Make a single opening only, disturbing the mother as little as possible, and put the tip of the tubing or the straw just beneath the mother — not all the way to the bottom of the container. That way, the liquid you're adding will have maximum contact with the film of *acetobacter*. In about a month, you'll have a strong, excellent vinegar.

Strain the liquid through a cloth, bottle the vinegar, and store it in a warm place for at least a month to allow it to age. The final product is a fine wine vinegar with the character of the wine ingredients you started with. If you'd like to enhance the flavor of the vinegar with your favorite herbs — tarragon is a perennial favorite — you need only bring the vinegar to a boil, add a sprig of fresh herb to the bottle, and pour the hot vinegar into the bottle — a little at a time to avoid breaking the glass. When the month has passed, the vinegar will have the subtle flavor of the herb. Once you've bottled your vinegar, clean the keg thoroughly. Then you're ready to begin again with a new set of leftovers from your next batch of wine.

USING WINE

If you aren't planning a new batch of wine, you can make vinegar from your existing wines. You'll need to fill the wooden container with a good-quality wine vinegar. You can use your own, or you can purchase a white wine vinegar and begin with that. (White wine vinegar will have the least effect on the flavor and color of the vinegar you make. If you're sure you want a red vinegar, you can use a red wine vinegar.)

We think some of the more interesting and flavorful wine vinegars we've made come from meads and metheglins. Since these wines don't have the same kind of leftover must that fruit wines do, this second method of vinegar making is the one we use for creating vinegars from meads and metheglins. You can also use other homemade wines (maybe those that don't please you for drinking) with this process.

Once you have a clean, dry, wooden container, you need to warm enough wine vinegar (to about 130°F.) to fill the keg or tub. This process will create the ideal conditions for *acetobacter* growth inside the container. After about 24 hours, two-thirds of this wine vinegar can be re-bottled. The remaining one-third remains in the keg to act as a starter for your next batch of vinegar.

Now you're ready to add the wine. Funnel the wine into the keg through the bung hole and allow it to sit for 8 to 10 days at room temperature. You will now have vinegar, but this first batch is usually fairly weak. To strengthen it, just remove a little liquid from the spigot and pour it back into the container through the bung hole, using a funnel and a piece of plastic tubing or a plastic drinking straw to pierce the mother. When the vinegar reaches the strength you want — you can tell by tasting it — bottle it and allow it to sit for about a month before using it. Scrub your vinegar keg, and you'll be ready to begin a new batch of vinegar whenever you choose.

You can leave about a third of your vinegar in the keg to act as a starter for your next batch of vinegar if you like. As long as you leave about one-third of the vinegar in the keg, with the mother, you can go on making vinegar indefinitely by just adding wine. But remember that the wine vinegar that's left in the container will affect the taste of the vinegar you make from that point on. If you make vinegar from a sage metheglin, for example, and then proceed to make one from a mead, the barest hint of sage will remain in the second batch of vinegar. If you're making herb vinegars, this interesting blending of flavors results in elusive tastes you may find delightful. If you're proceeding from a sage-metheglin vinegar to a vinegar made from a strawberry or raspberry wine, however, you might not find the flavor blending so appealing.

If you're lucky enough to have several vinegar-making kegs or tubs, and you want to use your creations for gift-giving or for making batches of pickles and preserves, which consume a lot of vinegar, then it's helpful to reserve one keg for herbal blends, one for fruit blends, and one for cider vinegar.

MAKING CIDER VINEGAR

Sweet cider vinegar is a fall favorite at our house, simply because it is such a natural and economical outgrowth of making apple pies, apple crunches, and apple cobblers this time of year. Using the leftover apple peelings and cores to make vinegar appeals to our sense of economy.

About the time we begin our first green-apple pies, we also start a batch of cider vinegar. We just take the peels and cores from a few tart apples, cover them with lukewarm water, and let them stand for a day or so. A foam begins to form along about the second day, and this is the beginning of the mother that ultimately turns apple cider into vinegar. If you let the peelings and cores soak for a week or two longer, you'll find that the remaining liquid is a fairly strong cider vinegar. Put this into your keg and add cider a little at a time, following the same process that you used for wine vinegar. Before long, you'll have a cask of cider vinegar.

We often add flavoring agents to our cider vinegars — chopped onions; garlic; herbs such as tarragon, thyme, sage, and basil; even ginger root for Oriental cuisine. If you make a light-colored cider vinegar, you might save some bottles until early the next summer and add the pretty purple blossoms of the chive plant for a decorative and slightly oniony cider vinegar. The light-colored vinegars are especially nice for this treatment because the blossoms give them just a hint of color that is very pretty in a cut-glass cruet.

We try to use only fresh herbs, because the fresh sprigs are so pretty in the bottle, but if you're willing to settle for the flavor without the pretty appearance, you can use dried herbs. You'll need to strain them out of the vinegar before bottling since they tend to crumble. If you happen to buy spices in clear glass bottles, the empties, filled with mild cider vinegar and a sprig of herb or a flower make lovely vinegar samplers. Fresh nasturtium blossoms in reds, oranges, and yellows impart an extra golden hue to vinegars. Put the little bottles of several varieties into a wooden spice rack and you'll have a lovely gift for a new bride or the older folks on your gift list. And hang a sampler in your own kitchen — folks will instantly recognize you as a gourmet cook.

The kinds of vinegar you make from homemade wines and ciders are limited only by your imagination. After you've made a few herbal varieties, new combinations with different flavoring agents and different kinds of wines will occur to you. In the meantime, here are a few special vinegars that you may want to try. *Bon appétit!*

AROMATIC VINEGAR

Make a mild vinegar from Lemon-Thyme Metheglin (page 69) or use any good-quality white wine vinegar. Take 1 quart of this vinegar and boil it until it is reduced to half its volume. While it's boiling, combine in a large bowl:

> 2 sprigs chives, chopped, *or* $1/2$ teaspoon dried
> 1 clove garlic, pressed
> 1 bay leaf
> 1 sprig thyme *or* $1/2$ teaspoon dried
> $1/2$ teaspoon freshly ground pepper
> $1/2$ teaspoon salt
> Fresh thyme

When the vinegar is ready, pour it into the bowl with the other ingredients and let stand for at least 2 hours. Then strain it through a cloth to remove the herb particles and use a funnel to pour into bottles. Add a sprig of fresh thyme to each bottle. Cover tightly when the vinegar is completely cool. This is a strong vinegar; we often add it to other wine vinegars to enhance their aroma — about 1 part Aromatic Vinegar to 2 parts of another kind.

RASPBERRY VINEGAR

This vinegar makes an excellent base for a variety of sweet-and-sour dishes. If you want to use it for this purpose, increase the sugar to 1 cup or the honey to 1/2 cup.

We also like to use it in fruit-salad dressings and in dips. A favorite for fruit cups is to mix the raspberry vinegar with cream cheese, poppy seed, and a little honey until it is of dressing consistency; then drizzle it over the fresh fruits for a colorful and delicious dressing. If you prefer a sweeter dressing, add a little more honey. You can also substitute other berries in this recipe — strawberry or blueberry vinegar is also delicious. Any berry wine works well as a basis for this vinegar.

Another use for raspberry vinegar, if your taste runs to more exotic dishes, is as an absolutely delectable fruit-salad dressing that is almost a dessert in itself. Use the sweeter version of the raspberry vinegar described above and drizzle it into a blender with almond butter, adding a little honey in a small stream until the mixture reaches the desired consistency. Then swirl it over your favorite fruit salad or use it as a dip for fresh strawberries, cantaloupe, and honeydew chunks.

Make a batch of vinegar from the must of Raspberry Melomel (page 58) or from the wine itself (if you can bear to part with it). You will need:

> 1 pint raspberries
> 2 cups raspberry melomel vinegar
> 2 teaspoons sugar *or* 1 teaspoon honey

Mash the berries and add the vinegar. Let the mixture stand for 4 days. Then add the sweetener and bring the mixture to a boil. Reduce the heat and simmer for 10–15 minutes. Strain and bottle, tightening the lids when the mixture is cool.

FIESTA VINEGAR

You can vary the "heat" of this vinegar by the variety of peppers you add. Jalapeño gives you a fiery variety, as does the tiny tabasco pepper. If you prefer a milder, "warm," version, try chopped anaheim peppers.

To make a delicious salad to accompany a variety of Mexican dishes, mix the vinegar with a little olive oil and drizzle over a salad made from 2 avocados, diced (not puréed); 1 tomato, seeded and diced; 1/2 medium onion, minced; and 1/2 teaspoon fresh mint leaves, minced. Serve the mixture on a bed of shredded lettuce and accompany it with tortilla chips that have been crisped for a few minutes in a moderate oven.

Begin this recipe with a wine vinegar made from Lemon-Thyme Metheglin (page 69) or use any good-quality white wine or mead vinegar. Bring a quart of the vinegar to a boil and reduce its volume by about a third. While the vinegar boils, combine the following ingredients in a large bowl:

1/2 cup chopped cilantro
1 teaspoon chopped chili pepper
1 teaspoon minced lemon zest
1/4 teaspoon salt
1 sprig mint, chopped

Pour the boiling vinegar into the bowl with the other ingredients and let the mixture sit for at least 2 hours. Strain and bottle. You may add a sprig of mint and a strip of lemon zest to the bottle.

SAVORY SALAD VINEGAR

Mixed with a little light oil, this vinegar is a cool delight with seafood salads. It is also a delightful component of homemade mayonnaise to use in tuna or salmon salads. For chicken salad, you may want to add just a whisper of honey to the final blend. Almond oil, Savory Salad Vinegar, and chopped cashews make a delightful dressing for chicken salad — and if you like your chicken with a Chinese flair, try adding these same ingredients to a wine vinegar made from Ginger Metheglin (page 66).

Make a light vinegar from Dry Apple Wine (page 17). Place it in a pan and boil until it is reduced by about one-fourth in volume. While the vinegar is boiling, put the following into a bowl:

1 clove garlic, pressed
2 umbels fresh dill *or* 2 tablespoons dried dill and 1/2
    teaspoon dried dill seed
2 sprigs fresh mint
1/4 teaspoon salt
1 teaspoon minced lemon zest

Pour the boiling vinegar into the bowl with the other ingredients and let the mixture sit for at least 2 hours. Strain and bottle. You may add a sprig of mint to the bottle. When the vinegar is completely cool, cap tightly.

9

Your Winemaking Questions Answered

Q. What is an acid blend and why do I need to add it to my wine?

A. The ideal wine has an acid content that is in balance with the tannins and sweetness of the wine. Some fruits that make an otherwise delicious wine are lacking in sufficient acid for good taste. When the acid component in the must is too low, fermentation is poor and the wine develops a mediciney taste. That's when adding an acid blend is important.

Most acid blends contain 1 part citric acid, 2 parts malic acid, and 3 parts tartaric acid. All of these are natural acids, found in various fruits. Fruits rich in citric acid include most of the citrus fruits, currants, strawberries, raspberries, and tangerines. Since citric acid also adds a nice fruitiness and brilliance to the wine, some winemakers routinely use citrus juice as their only acid component. Those who opt for acid blend, including malic acid and tartaric acid, say that these two acids help to speed fermentation and improve the vinous character of the wine. Malic acid is found naturally in apples, apricots, blackberries, dark cherries, plums, gooseberries, nectarines, and rhubarb. Tartaric acid usually comes from grapes.

Q. How do I know which fruits are high or low in acid and how much acid or acid blend to add?

A.   Acid can be measured through a process called *titration*, and some winemaking suppliers sell kits for that purpose; but we think the process is complicated and probably not worth the effort for folks who make wine at home. Some winemakers use litmus paper and compare the color of the strip to a prepared chart. But because there are other things in wine besides acid components that affect the measurement, the litmus test is probably not much more accurate than just tasting the wine and adjusting accordingly. As you become a more experienced winemaker and taster, you'll become surprisingly good at judging whether you need to add additional acid. In the meantime, rely on the supplier's directions in relation to the amount of acids in your ingredients.

Generally speaking, flowers and vegetables have little acid of their own and wines made from these ingredients need about 2 teaspoons of acid added per gallon. To help you estimate how acid your ingredients are, look at which ingredients fall into the low, medium, and high acid levels on the chart below:

Low Acid	Medium Acid	High Acid
beets	apples	blackberries
dates	apricots	gooseberries
figs	cherries	loganberries
rose hips, petals	grapes	quinces
flowers	juice concentrates	raspberries
herbs	plums	strawberries
dried fruits	nectarines	most citrus
elderberries	oranges	currants
pears	peaches	rhubarb
	tangerines	

Q.   What are Campden tablets exactly, and what are they for?

A.   A Campden tablet contains about 7 grains of potassium metabisulfite. When you dissolve a tablet in any slightly acid solution, such as wine must, it releases approximately 4 grains of sulfur dioxide. At that rate, one tablet in a gallon of wine results in about 60 parts per million of sulfur dioxide. It's an effective sterilizing agent at that rate because it stops the growth of wild yeasts and spoilage organisms but doesn't affect the taste of the wine except to make it marginally more acid, which is almost always a plus. See pages 13–14 and 16 for more information.

Q. What causes cloudy wine, and how can I get my wines to clear?

A. Wines become cloudy for a number of reasons. First, if you disturb the sediment at the bottom of the container when you rack the wine, some of the suspended particles might be mixed back into the wine. If this happens, an additional racking several days later, taking care to leave the sediment undisturbed, is all that's required to clear the wine. Wines that clear naturally, with careful racking, are always better than wines that overzealous home winemakers have tried to clear by filtering them through filter paper (such as coffee filters) or aquarium charcoal filters. We don't recommend filtering because in addition to sediment, the process often removes other components of the wine, such as its elusive bouquet, subtle flavor, or characteristic color. And it often exposes the wine to additional air, which can lead to oxidation and spoilage.

Sometimes wines remain stubbornly murky, and in that case the culprit is usually pectin, starch, or protein in the wine. Most of the recipes in this book call for pectic enzyme because it is much easier to prevent pectin cloudiness than to cure it. Similarly, another enzyme, *amylozyme,* will turn starch, which can't be fermented, into sugar, which can. Treating your wine with this enzyme will clear it if starch is the problem. Protein cloudiness is usually treated by *fining* — using a substance such as Bentonite to clear the wine. Fining usually requires a rather exact dosage based on the amount of protein in the wine and for that reason is not frequently used by amateur winemakers.

Our ancestors had an inexact but rather effective way of dealing with cloudy wine. They dried a broken eggshell for a few seconds in the oven and dropped it into the wine. The use of eggshells is based on a sound principle. Modern commercial wineries often include albumin among their collection of fining agents. Some of that substance may remain on the eggshell, and the shell itself absorbs impurities — sometimes, unfortunately, including color. If all else fails, you might want to try the eggshell treatment, just as Grandpa did.

Q. My wines never seem to be quite as sweet as I'd like them to be. What can I do to get the sweetness I like?

A. Wines continue to ferment and turn sugar into alcohol and carbon dioxide until the wine reaches a point at which the alcohol is concentrated enough that it prevents the yeast from growing any further—usually 14–18 percent alcohol. Once this point is reached, what sugar hasn't been converted to alcohol and carbon dioxide remains to sweeten the wine. If you taste the wine once it has stopped fermenting, and it is too dry, it is likely that the fermentation process has used up the sugars present and stopped when this source of energy ran out. You can add additional sugar at this point either by dissolving sugar in a little of the wine and adding the mixture back into the fermentation vessel or by adding a simple syrup, made by dissolving sugar in boiling water, cooling it, and adding it to the wine. If the wine begins fermenting again, it had not reached its highest concentration of alcohol, and it will use up some of the sugar you've added to resume the fermentation process. By adding a little sugar at a time, monitoring the fermentation process, and tasting at intervals, you should be able to adjust the sweetness of your wine to exactly suit your taste.

Keep careful records of how much you add, and don't add too much at a time. When you have the perfect combination, adjust your recipe to suit your taste for the next batch of wine.

Q. How does yeast work to make wine?

A. Yeast is really a single-celled plant that grows in sugary solutions and in the process produces alcohol and carbon dioxide in about equal parts. Yeast cells accomplish this conversion of sugar to alcohol by producing enzymes that "digest" the sugars. Eventually they produce enough alcohol that it's lethal to the yeast cells themselves, and they fall to the bottom of the winemaking vessel as *lees*, or sediment. Because different kinds of yeast cells have different tolerances for the amount of alcohol that will ultimately kill them, the kind of yeast you use will help determine how potent your wine will be.

Yeasts need certain conditions to grow and reproduce favorably: warmth, oxygen, sugar, nitrogenous matter, vitamins, and acid. But because yeast is so important to the winemaking process, the suppliers of wine yeasts actually grow the most genetically efficient strains for use by winemakers. That's one of the reasons we prefer purchasing good-quality wine yeast for our winemaking. It's a little like purchasing hybrid seed for your garden because it guarantees healthier, better adapted plants.

Q. How do I know which kinds of wine yeasts to buy?

A. Wine yeasts come from the skins of grapes, with each variety of grape having a slightly different variety of yeast. These yeasts are collected and cultured and sold by the packet. A good rule of thumb in choosing wine yeasts is to look at the kind of grape wine that each yeast makes. You'll find yeasts for port, sherry, Tokay, Madeira, Malaga, Sauternes, and Burgundy among others. If you are making a dark red wine — from elderberries or blackberries, for example — you'll probably want to choose a yeast that makes a dark red grape wine, like port or Burgundy. We like to use a champagne yeast for honey wines because we like the taste. Since wine yeasts are relatively inexpensive and you can extend what you buy by making your own yeast starter-cultures, we suggest that you experiment — it's part of the fun of making your own wines!

Q. Can I use the yeast I buy at the supermarket to make wine?

A. A lot of old-time winemakers used bread yeasts to make wines because that was what was available, and you can make a number of acceptable wines by that method. Bread yeasts are from the same family as wine yeasts, but they *are* a different variety. If you experiment with making wines with both kinds of yeast, you'll notice two major differences — besides the difference in flavor. First, wine yeasts don't bubble as much or as energetically in the first fermentation. This more subdued bubbling means that fewer fragrance elements are carried off with the carbon dioxide, so wines made with wine yeast tend to have better bouquets. Second, wine yeasts tend to leave firmer sediment at the bottom of your fermentation vessel. That makes racking easier, since you're less likely to stir up sediment inadvertently when you rack the wine.

Q. What is pectic enzyme and why do you add it to wine?

A. Generally speaking, *enzymes* are naturally occurring substances that aid plants and animals in breaking down complex substances such as sugars and starches into simpler forms. Pectic enzyme helps to break down *pectin*, a complex molecule found in many fruits, into simple sugars. When you add pectic enzyme to your wine recipes, then, you are making sure that any pectin that's present in the fruits you've used for your wine is turned into sugars, which fermentation will turn into alcohol and carbon dioxide. Not only will you have a more complete fermentation using pectic enzyme, but you'll also have a clearer, more brilliant wine.

Q. Whenever I read an article on wines, I'm confused about some of the terms the writers use. Can you define some of the common terms that wine writers use to describe wines — like *body* and *bouquet*, for example? And what is a *foxy* wine?

A. If you've ever watched winetasters in action, you'll notice that they go through a precise ritual whenever they taste a wine. First, they hold the wine glass up to the light to look at the color and clarity. They may swirl the wine in the glass and hold it under their nose to enjoy the *bouquet* — the perfume of the wine that's part of the enjoyment of savoring wines. They may also look to see if a bit of the wine clings to the sides of the glass — if it has what tasters call "legs" that seem to climb a ways up the side of the glass and are a somewhat inexact gauge of a wine's alcohol content. A wine's viscosity, or *body*, is evaluated partly by looking at the sides of the glass and partly by the way the wine feels in the mouth. As you start to look for these things in your own wines, you'll notice quite a variability in body, depending on the kind of wine you've made.

Once winetasters have looked at and smelled the wine, they're ready to taste it. Good wines are generally "balanced" in their taste — with sweet wines, for example, needing a bit more acid and perhaps a bit more tannin, to balance the sugar. Most of the terms used to describe taste are self-explanatory — fruity, light, heavy, resinous, as well as sweet, semi-sweet, semi-dry, dry, and brut (very dry). *Foxy* is a term often applied to wines made from American grape varieties, because some of these make a wine with the easily recognizable "grape" taste that we learned to recognize in grape soda and grape jelly. Those "wine experts" who are eager to tell us what wines "should" taste like often see foxiness in wine as a fault — a mark of inferior quality. But as more and more people become familiar with the variety of wines available — both imported and domestic — they've also become more confident wine drinkers. A good wine is one that pleases the drinker, whether it's a foxy grape wine or a mellow cherry melomel.

Q. Should fresh fruit be washed before you begin the wine-making process?

A. Old-time winemakers who made wine only from grapes, allowing the natural yeast on the skins to begin the fermentation process, were often reluctant to remove the "bloom" or naturally occurring yeasts on the grapes because it was essential to the fermentation process. But times and conditions have changed drastically since the early winemakers grew grapes without sprays and in air that was free from environmental pollutants. Now, yeasts are added to the must, and the only reason for not washing fruits thoroughly is gone.

We suggest that you place whatever fruit you're going to use in a colander and run cool water over it for several minutes before you begin winemaking. Washing fruit later in the process, after stems and pits have been removed, results in a loss of fruit juices.

Q. I've tried a few wine recipes that call for citrus peels, and they've always had a bitter taste. What am I doing wrong?

A. If you look carefully at citrus fruit when you peel it, you'll notice that an orange, for example, has a thin orange rind, then a white fibrous substance (the inner rind), and then the pulp of the fruit, in that order. If you taste the white substance beneath the orange rind, you'll find a rather bland-tasting part of the citrus. But if that same bland substance is added to wine must and allowed to sit as the fermentation continues for several days, a bitter component is released in your wine. If you peel the fruit before you begin making wine, this white inner rind adheres to the essential-oil-rich

rich outer rind, and it's very difficult to separate the two. We've found that the best method for removing the citrus zest, or outer rind, is to use a vegetable peeler and remove it before peeling the orange. A fine grater also works well if you don't grate too deeply. Then remove the white inner rind as you would if the orange part was still attached, and discard it. That should eliminate the bitter taste in your wine.

Q. Can wine bottles be reused? What about the corks? I've bought some wines that have screw caps. Can I reuse the bottles and the caps?

A. Wine bottles can be reused as long as you're careful to sterilize them beforehand. The same is true for corks; you can sterilize corks in a solution of 1 Campden tablet dissolved in a gallon of water, or by scalding them *briefly* with boiling water. In our experience, corks that are sterilized with bleach or by lengthy boiling absorb either the taste of the bleach or a good deal of water. Corks that have gone "fat" with absorbed water are next to impossible to insert in bottles. Since corks are cheap and readily available, we recommend that you use new corks whenever you make wine.

The screw caps on bottles are usually sealed as well as tightened. If you reuse a screw cap and it leaks air for the time that your wine is aging, you may find that you've been "penny-wise and pound-foolish" because your wine may oxidize, or turn to vinegar. For the few pennies that new corks cost, they are well worth the investment.

Q. What is the best way to cork wine bottles?

A. If you make wine in small quantities, it is probably not economical to invest in corking equipment, and there really is no need to do so. Just make sure your bottles and corks are sterile and of compatible sizes. Insert the cork a little way into the bottle, put a couple of thicknesses of heavy cardboard over it (to avoid chipping the bottle neck), and tap it into place with a mallet. Some winemakers tell us that they put the cork into the bottle as far as they can with hand pressure and then put the cork against the wall and push. Never discount muscle power!

Q. What are jug wines?

A. Any wine that is bottled in half-gallon or one-gallon containers — usually jugs with a single or double handle — is properly called a "jug wine." Since it is more profitable to bottle fine vintage wines in the traditional 25-ounce wine bottle, the term "jug wine" has come to connote a cheaper or inferior wine. In some cases, that is an unfair designation, since there are a number of perfectly acceptable jug wines. When you bottle your own country wines, the designation becomes academic. If you entertain frequently and would normally consume more than one 25-ounce bottle of wine in the course of an evening's entertainment, by all means bottle your country wine in jugs. Just remember that wines are more prone to oxidize, or "turn," once they are opened, so bottle your wines in quantities that are likely to be consumed in a single setting.

Q. I made a batch of rhubarb wine, and mold grew on the top of the must. Is this harmful, and if it happens again, should I throw the whole batch away?

A. Sterilizing your must with a Campden tablet (see pages 132–133) will usually prevent mold, but if you don't want to have sulfites in your wine, or if you don't keep the must completely covered during the first fermentation, mold might grow on a cap if it is exposed to airborne molds. Generally speaking, this mold is not harmful and you don't have to discard the wine. But you do need to be careful when you punch a hole in the cap to let oxygen into the must that you don't mix the mold into the wine. Depending on the composition, it could give your wine an off flavor.

Q. Do wine bottles have to be filled to the top? I always seem to end up with one half-filled bottle when I syphon wine into bottles, and I don't know what to do with it.

A. It's always a good idea to keep air from your wine once it has completed the first, rapid fermentation. Otherwise, the wine could oxidize or turn to vinegar. If you end up with a partial bottle of wine when you're bottling, there are several things you can do. The easiest way to handle the problem is by "topping-off." You simply take the remaining wine, add enough of a simple syrup (made by boiling 1 part sugar with 3 parts water) to fill the last bottle, and return the mixture to an airlocked fermentation vessel until it stops fermenting. Then bottle the resulting wine. If you'd rather not bother with the topping-off process, you can add the leftover wine to another compatible batch, or add the leftover quantity to your vinegar cask, or sample a bit of your new wine early.

Q. Is it harmful to age your wine right in the fermentation vessel as long as you keep the airlock on the container?

A. Some winemakers never bottle their wines. They simply leave the finished wine in an airlocked fermentation vessel until they're ready to serve it and then syphon the appropriate quantity into a carafe. That way they're never faced with the "what-do-I-do-with-a-half-bottle-of-wine" dilemma. The problem with handling your wine this way is that you need a number of large containers and whenever you want to make more wine you need to locate additional fermentation vessels. Sometimes big containers are more difficult to store than smaller ones, too. And wine is more likely to oxidize in large containers if it's not used fairly quickly, because every time you remove wine from a container, it is replaced with air. Choose whatever method of storage fits your lifestyle and storage capabilities.

Q. Why do you stir the must for several days to introduce oxygen into the wine and then put it into an airlocked vessel to keep oxygen out?

A. During the first fermentation, the yeast in your wine grows rapidly, using oxygen and producing alcohol and carbon dioxide. But the level to which the yeast can grow in the presence of air is limited by the amount of alcohol in the mixture. Aerobic fermentation proceeds until the concentration of alcohol stops the process, leaving a lot of unused sugar in the must and your wine sticky sweet and vulnerable to spoilage. Once the container is airlocked, however, the yeast switches to a new mode of growth, one in which more alcohol is produced — a condition that is tolerated by the yeasts once oxygen is no longer present. Aerobic fermentation alone will not produce enough alcohol to ensure that the wine will keep well. Thus both processes are necessary for good aging and keeping qualities — and of course, good taste.

Q. What are yeast nutrients, and why do you add them to wines?

A. Yeasts need certain organic compounds to grow and reproduce efficiently, just as all plants and animals do. Most of the time, wines made with fruit have these organic nutrients because the fruit provides them. But some wines, especially those made with honey, are lacking in these compounds. If you fail to provide them in some way, the yeast will grow for awhile and then quit, just as plants will turn yellow and quit growing if nitrogen is absent in the soil, or humans will fail to thrive without essential vitamins. When yeast stops growing, the wine never reaches its full alcohol potential, and it becomes vulnerable to spoilage. Since it's difficult to measure just how much of each nutrient may be present in the must, we generally add yeast nutrient as a kind of insurance policy against "malnutrition," just as mothers sometimes give their children vitamins "just in case." Even in those kinds of wine that have essential growth nutrients, fermentation is often faster and more efficient if yeast nutrients are added.

Yeast nutrients may contain any of the following: ammonium sulfate, magnesium sulfate, potassium phosphate, diammonium phosphate, ammonium chloride, and thiamine. Most of these substances are available from your pharmacist or are sold as yeast nutrients — often a blend of several — through suppliers of winemaking equipment. We often use them because they're quick and easy, but if you've formulated your wines — primarily flower and honey wines — with juices to supply these nutrients, you won't need them at all.

Q. Can you process wines in canning jars like you do fruits and vegetables?

A. Some commercial winemakers do pasteurize wines — though not at canner temperatures — to improve their shipping and keeping qualities. This is rarely done with vintage varieties, however. For the home winemaker, processing wines as you might canned goods isn't recommended. First of all, it's not necessary, since the alcohol in your wine is an effective preservative and your homemade wine will not be shipped and jostled and subjected to a variety of temperature conditions. But even more important, processing wine in a hot-water bath or pressure cooker will almost surely result in some if not all of the alcohol evaporating, since alcohol boils at a lower temperature than water. Finally, vintage winemakers don't pasteurize their wines because they know that fine wines are alive. The aging process that mellows and refines a wine would stop if the wine were subjected to high temperatures. Make sure to keep your equipment and bottling supplies sterile, and you'll have no need for further processing.

Q. Why do most wine books tell you to store wine on its side?

A. Most home winemakers use corks when they bottle their wines, and corks can dry out and shrink over long periods of time in storage. When you store wine bottles on their sides with the mouth of the bottle slightly lower than the bottom, the cork is kept moist and swollen, preventing air from seeping into the bottle and causing oxidization or acetification (wine turning to vinegar).

Q. A lot of old-time wine recipes call for raisins. Is there any reason for adding raisins to wine recipes using other fruits?

A. Once you remember that raisins are dried grapes, you can see why so many country wine recipes call for them. Chances are that raisins have a trace of yeast remaining on their skins even after the drying process, which is important if no other source of yeast is available. Too, raisins and grapes give wine a vinous quality, even if it is primarily flavored with another fruit. And raisins contribute grape sugar, tannins, and flavor to the finished wine. No wonder so many old-time recipes call for raisins.

Q. Some wine recipes call for boiling some of the ingredients in a non-aluminum pan. Why is that? Are there other kinds of containers that I shouldn't use in winemaking?

A. Because wines and wine musts are essentially acid, they can react with metals to form metal salts, some of which are toxic to humans. It's a good idea to stay away from aluminum or copper pans when you're making wines; stainless steel, glass, or unchipped enamel pans are fine. Be careful, too, of the containers you use for

---

fermentation vessels. Most crocks made in the United States are free from harmful metals, but large crocks from other countries may be finished with glazes containing metals such as lead that will leach into the wine. Some sources believe that lead-poisoned wine, contaminated from storage containers, contributed to the decline of the Roman empire, because lead-poisoning causes a decrease in mental acuity. Finally, although plastics are generally inert materials that don't react with wine, we try to stay away from colored plastic vessels because we're not sure whether dyes will affect the quality or flavor of wines. White or clear-plastic containers are easy to clean and sterilize and, psychologically, they feel cleaner.

Q. What is a *hydrometer* and how is it used in winemaking?

A. A *hydrometer* looks rather like a thermometer in a glass tube. It is weighted on one end so that it will float upright in a liquid. You can take a reading where the main surface of the liquid cuts the scale and use that reading to determine how much sugar is in fruit juices (or in your must) and how much sugar you need to add to make a wine of the strength you want. A hydrometer will also let you keep track of a wine's progress as the sugar content goes down and the alcohol percentage increases. And when the fermentation is finished, it will let you figure out the strength of the

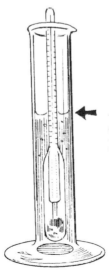

A hydrometer reading is taken at the point on the scale intersected by the surface of the liquid.

finished wine. Most companies that sell winemaking supplies have hydrometers especially for winemakers. A hydrometer will even tell you when it's safe to bottle your wine without worrying about cork popping or breakage.

Q. How can I tell if my wine is spoiled?

A. Several different kinds of bacteria can make wine spoil. The best known, of course, *acetobacter*, turns wine to vinegar, and it's not difficult to figure out when that has happened — one whiff is usually enough. Wine often turns to vinegar when the must is contaminated (usually by bacteria-carrying fruitflies) during the first fermentation. But sometimes wine doesn't turn to vinegar when it spoils, so the characteristic odor isn't present. By and large, though, bad wine smells bad and looks bad. If it has started to oxidize, you'll usually notice a brownish color and a bit of scum floating on the surface. Although a wine that has started to "turn" can be salvaged for vinegar, an oxidized wine should be discarded.

Q. What if I add the wrong amount of water to the first fermentation container?

A. You're always going to be guessing a little at the amount of water to add, and if you end up with a little more or less than a gallon of wine, it isn't really too significant. Too little can be topped off with a sugar syrup (see pages 139–140) if you want to keep the vessel full; if you have more than a gallon of wine and you're using a gallon container for the second fermentation, the excess can be discarded or saved for another yeast starter-culture — you can even freeze the juice and use it in a subsequent batch.

Q. A few years ago sulfites on fresh fruits and vegetables, at salad bars, and in wine and beer got a lot of publicity. Can you explain how sulfites are used in wines and how they function?

A. Wine sterilizing agents such as Campden tablets release sulfur dioxide when you add them to must or wine, and that gas kills off any unwanted yeast. After 24 hours pass, the gas is gone, but some sulfur residue (a minute amount) remains in the wine. If you add another Campden tablet to stabilize your wine once fermentation is complete, a bit more sulfur, in the form of sulfites, or sulfur salts, stays in the wine. These sulfite preservatives are usually unde-tectable in wine, and, unless you are allergic to them, they cause no ill effects.

Until a few years ago, sulfur was routinely used to preserve dried fruits, fresh fruits, and vegetables in produce departments in super-markets and on the fresh foods in salad bars. But some allergic reactions in sensitive people caused additional regulation of sul-fites because there was no way for people who were allergic to them to know if they were present until it was too late. As with certain other allergies, a tiny percent of the population has a severe reac-tion and may go into shock if sulfites are consumed. For most sulfite-sensitive people, though, too much sulfite results in a stuffy nose for a few hours. Almost all commercially bottled wines have some sulfites; if you're allergic to them, omit them from your wines, and you should be able to sip your country wines without any adverse reactions.

Q. How does a fermentation trap or airlock work?

A. Made of glass or plastic, fermentation locks are usually composed of a tube that has been bent into either a U shape or a cup shape and works a little like the trap under your kitchen sink. One end of the tube fits into a cork or rubber stopper that is placed in the neck of a jug or other fermentation vessel. The other end is free so that carbon dioxide can escape from the vessel. A little water stays in the cup or bend of the lock to keep air from going back into the must. As carbon dioxide is created by the fermentation process, pressure builds up until it's strong enough to move the water out of the way and a "burp" of gas bubbles out. Some winemakers add a little sulfite to the water in the trap so it can't be contaminated with bacteria that might turn the wine to vinegar.

Q. What does the term *lees* refer to?

A. *Lees* are the residue that collects in the bottom of a vessel or bottle containing wine. If you bottle your wine too early, or if you are careless in racking your finished wine into the bottle, you might find a bit of residue in the bottom of your wine bottles. If that happens, you can rack the wine into another bottle and re-cork or, if you discover lees at serving time, rack the wine into a carafe.

Q. What does the term "stuck wine" mean? What's the cure?

A. Winemakers say wine is stuck if the fermentation stops before the optimum amount of sugar is converted to alcohol, so that the wine is oversweet and, if you measure with a hydrometer (see page 143), the specific gravity (see Glossary, page 163) is too high. Fermentation can stop for several reasons: Maybe the temperature is too low or too high. Maybe you inadvertently added too much sugar and the wine has reached its limit of alcohol tolerance. It may be that some organic nutrient is missing. If the wine "sticks" during the first fermentation, it may be lacking in oxygen. If the same thing happens during subsequent fermentations, the carbon dioxide may have become too concentrated and caused the wine yeast to stop growing.

If the problem is with temperature, you can usually restart the fermentation by moving the vessel to a warmer or cooler spot and adding a little starter-culture, just for good measure. If you've simply added too much sugar, dilute the mixture with water or juice so that the alcohol content is reduced and fermentation can resume. If you didn't add a yeast nutrient to your starter-culture, you may need to give your wine a little vitamin lift, either by adding some yeast nutrient to a small container of the wine and then adding it back to the must, or by adding just the tip of a teaspoon of epsom salts or 3 mg. of vitamin B_1 (thiamine). If all of these remedies fail, you'll probably need to solve the problem one step at a time. Just make a $1/2$ pint of starter-culture and when it's working well, add an equal amount of the stuck wine. Wait until this mixture starts to ferment and repeat the process until all of your stuck wine has been added and the whole batch is actively fermenting.

Q. What are tannins and why are they added to some wine recipes?

A. Wines that have no tannins are generally dull and flat. But if you've ever tasted wine that draws your mouth into a pucker — usually a dark red one — you know that too much tannin can make a wine bitter and astringent-tasting as well. As with most wine elements, the trick is to balance the tannins with the other ingredients. Tannins are naturally occurring substances that are present in some fruits, in the membranes between nutmeats in some varieties of nuts (especially hickory nuts), and in tea. In those recipes in which we've added tannin, it's because the wine seemed a bit characterless, probably because the particular set of ingredients was lacking in this essential element. If you find that your wine seems to lack character or zest, you can add tannin (or a tablespoon of strong tea to a gallon of wine), and you'll be surprised at the improvement.

Q. Most recipes in this book call for yeast starter-cultures. Why not just add the yeast directly to the wine?

A. We like to use a yeast starter-culture for a couple of reasons. First, as mentioned on page 15, since a yeast starter-culture is prepared ahead of time — usually 1 to 3 hours before you add it to the wine — the yeast is already actively growing and fermentation of the must starts immediately. We think that gives us fresher-tasting wines. Second, starter-cultures conserve wine yeast, and if you use an all-purpose one, such as an orange-juice culture, you can keep it going, much as pioneer cooks — and some modern ones — kept a sourdough starter going, through several batches of wine. Just add more juice and nutrients to a little of the culture that's left — about 1/2 cup — and keep it in the refrigerator until a couple of hours before you'll need it. Then bring it into a warm room and wait for fermentation to begin. Although a sourdough starter can be kept for years, we don't recommend keeping your starter-culture too long — perhaps just over the course of a summer's winemaking. The possibility of contamination with airborne wild yeasts as the bottle is opened and closed always exists. Finally, we use a yeast starter-culture because it reduces the possibility of having a stuck fermentation (see page 146), since the yeast is already viable and actively growing in a starter-culture.

Q. Are there such things as "no-yeast" recipes for wine?

A. Some winemakers make wine with nothing but grapes, but only because grapes already have yeast on their skins and some of this yeast gets the fermentation process going. In most cases, though, the country wines in this book are made without grapes and must have yeast to ferment. Even those recipes that do have grapes or raisins might not have the best yeast for the job, so don't try to save a few cents on yeast; in the long run, you may end up wasting all the other ingredients in your wine, which may have to be discarded.

Q.   Is it okay to use refined sugar in winemaking?

A.   Almost all the recipes in this book use refined sugar, except for the honey-based wines. We've never found any discernible difference among most sugars in taste, fermentability, or keeping quality. Since refined sugar is abundant and inexpensive, we think it's the best option for country winemakers. One or two recipes in this book call for brown sugar — mostly for the taste, appropriate to a particular wine.

Q.   Some recipes call for adding the sugar in stages. Others add it all at once. Why?

A.   Sometimes too much sugar can overwhelm the yeast in the must, just as too much alcohol can, and fermentation has a hard time getting started, or it gets stuck (see page 146). If we have found that to be a problem, we've specified adding the sugar in stages. Some winemakers do that routinely, as a kind of insurance policy, and there's no harm in doing so. We think using a yeast starter-culture is also a kind of insurance against slow start-ups — and it requires less fooling around with the must and less record-keeping than adding sugar in stages.

Q.   Does it make any difference what kind of water I use when I make wine?

A.   For the most part, any pure water is satisfactory for winemaking. We use tap water, but we usually bring it to a boil for a few minutes, either because the recipe calls for boiling or because boiling drives off any chlorine that remains in the water. If your water is very hard, you may want to use distilled water in your winemaking, since the minerals have been removed. Since softened water usually has sodium salts, we don't recommend using softened water in winemaking. Some winemakers think that softened water also alters the taste of the wine.

Q. How important is temperature when wine is going through the fermentation process? Can I speed it up by using heat?

A. Your wine will bubble along happily at the same temperatures that make you comfortable, although most experts put the best temperature for fermentation at about 60–65°F. The only time it might be appropriate to add heat to the process is if you're making wine in an unheated porch or outbuilding or in a very cool basement. In that case, a heating pad under your fermenting wine will keep the process perking along. But heating the must to higher temperatures in hopes of speeding up the winemaking process is sure to backfire. Get it too warm and the yeast will stop growing or die. Then, if you hope to salvage your ingredients at all, you must start at the beginning again, adding a yeast starter-culture and waiting. Finally, a "too energetic" fermentation usually means that some of the aromatic parts of the wine — the parts that give it its bouquet — are bubbled off with the carbon dioxide. The result is that your wine has much less bouquet than if you fermented it at a cooler temperature. If you happen to have a wine in a warm spot that is fermenting very energetically during its primary fermentation, just sniff. If you smell your bouquet disappearing in the bubbles, you'll probably want to move your wine to a cooler spot, even if the fermentation takes longer. Waiting is what really good winemakers do best.

Q. What is the best way to get the juice out of the fruit I use for winemaking?

A. There are almost as many ways to extract fruit juice as there are winemakers who want to do it. In pioneer times, when equipment of any kind was hard to come by, winemakers fermented their wines on the pulp of chopped or mashed fruit, introducing the yeast right away, and draining the juice off a week or 10 days later. If color and pulp were important in the recipe, they sometimes put the solids into a jelly bag or wrapped them in cheesecloth and either squeezed the juices out or let gravity extract them by hanging the jelly bag over a crock or bucket.

In Europe, French, German, and Italian winemakers preferred pressing, and some winepresses were large enough that horses

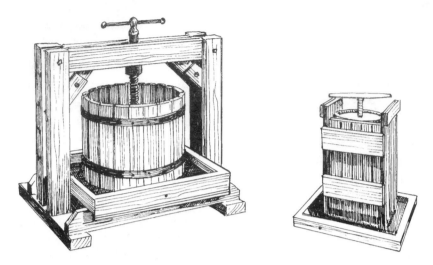

Large and small fruit presses are available, but a small one meets the needs of most home winemakers.

provided the...well, the horsepower to operate the presses. Country winemakers who want to make wines at home don't really need massive presses. Small, wooden fruit presses work well for fruits like grapes and berries, which must be broken, or apples, which hold their juice rather firmly. You simply wrap the chopped fruit in cheesecloth and turn the wheel at the top to apply increasing pressure to the fruit. You'll soon have a good quantity of fresh fruit juice. You can buy one of these small fruit presses for under $100, and they're so sturdy they'll last for years. Don't rush the pressing, and be careful not to crush seeds or pips, as they'll give your wine an off flavor.

Some wine recipes call for boiling the fruit or vegetables and then draining off the juice. Use this method with care and be careful not to overcook, or you may have trouble getting your wine to clear.

Finally, many winemakers simply chop or crush the fruit and pour boiling water over it to remove the juice and flavor. This method has the added advantage of killing off most of the wild yeasts and bacteria, so you may not need to add sulfites to your must. Probably the greater portion of our country-wine recipes use this method.

Q. I'm afraid of exploding wine bottles. What are some ways to ensure that I've waited long enough before bottling my wine?

A. If you have a hydrometer (see page 143), you can use it to measure the alcohol content and amount of sugar in your wine before bottling, so you can be sure that fermentation is complete. But most amateur winemakers who don't have special equipment routinely take other precautions to ensure against exploding bottles. If you aren't sure that fermentation is complete, move your wine to a warm room and watch for bubbles, especially along the sides of the container. If no bubbles appear in 24 hours, your wine is finished. If you see any bubbles, wait 2 weeks to a month and test again. When you don't see any more bubbles, put the wine into bottles, but don't cap them tightly for several days. Some country winemakers put a balloon over the bottle neck and watch to see if carbon dioxide causes the balloon to inflate. If that should happen, there's no need to return the wine to an airlocked vessel; just let the balloon act as an airlock, and wait until it stops getting bigger before you cork the wine. Finally, if you put the cork only about a quarter of the way into the bottle and the fermentation is still going on, you might get some cork-popping, but your bottles won't break. If everything is okay after several days, tap the corks all the way into the bottles and store them in a cool wine cellar or other location.

Q. I can't seem to get my wine to syphon from one container to another. What are some tips for easy racking?

A. First of all, make sure that you've set everything up in advance. It's pretty disconcerting to get a tube of wine flowing and then discover that you can't reach the container you wanted to rack the wine into. We usually up-end a bucket on the counter top and set the container we'll be racking *from* on the bucket. Then we set the container we'll be racking *to* in the sink. That makes the bottom of the first container about even with the top of the second one. Now insert your tube or syphon into the wine, making sure that you don't put the tube all the way to the bottom, where it will pick up sediment. Suck on the other end of the tube much as you would on a drinking straw. You'll get a taste of wine, and it will keep flowing as long as you lower that end of the tube so that it's below the end in the container of wine to be racked. Quickly place the free end of the tube into the container in the sink (you may want to use a funnel for containers with narrow openings), and the wine should continue to flow until either you remove the tube or enough wine is syphoned into the second container so that the end is no longer in the wine in the first container. You may get a little spillage, especially if you are syphoning from a larger container into several smaller bottles. That's why we put the containers we're syphoning into in the sink!

Q. I notice that in a couple of recipes straining is called for instead of racking at an early stage. Can straining be substituted for racking in any recipe?

A. Using a strainer to remove the big pieces of fruit, skins, etc., is sometimes okay in very early stages of fermentation. But for wines further along in the process, racking reduces the contact with oxygen — which may aid in forming vinegar should any bacteria be present. Too, those wines that are further along in the process will be clearer with racking because not only are the big pieces removed, but the little stuff that makes for cloudy wines — dead yeast cells, minute fruit particles, etc. — will have settled to the bottom of the container and will be left behind. Finally, straining may seem easier if you haven't done it, but racking is really very simple. It takes a little bit longer for the wine to run through the tube, but it's better for the wine. And once you find a wine you like enough to make a large quantity, you'll find it darn near impossible to lift bigger containers and dump them through a strainer without a lot of splashing and sloshing.

Q. The winemaking process covers a lot of time. How can I be sure I'll remember when I'm supposed to accomplish all the steps in the process?

A. Anybody can make a good country wine once in a while. But winemakers who make consistently excellent wines do so because they keep consistently excellent records. The easiest way to do that is to keep a calendar — the kind with big squares for each day so you can write on it — just for winemaking. When you start a batch of wine, or even before you start, count out the number of days, weeks, or months that various stages should take and mark them on your calendar — in pencil. Wine is a living thing, and like all living things, it sometimes seems to march to a different beat than the one we'd planned. If your calendar tells you to rack your Cherry Melomel into bottles on January 5, for example, and it simply isn't ready to be racked, erase your notation and adjust it as often as necessary, so that your winemaking calendar for the year reflects not what you thought you would do, but what you actually did. You'll find this information very useful when you make your next batch of Cherry Melomel. Similarly, if you make any adjustments in ingredients, if your wine sticks (see page 146), if you find it necessary to add tea or sugar or additional acid, make note of those changes and adjust your recipe accordingly the next time you make that kind of wine.

If you have more than one kind of wine going at once, buy a supply of sticky labels at a stationery store and label each fermentation vessel with the name of the wine and the date you perform each operation. That way you won't start racking your Mulberry Wine when you're supposed to be racking your Raspberry Melomel. Keeping records may not be the most entertaining part of winemaking, but you'll be glad you kept them when some original recipe tastes so good that you just can't wait to make it again.

Q. What is a *malo-lactic* fermentation?

A. Once in a while, wine will undergo a third fermentation after it has been bottled — not the energetic kind that results in broken bottles, but a gentle fermentation that converts malic acid (found in apple juice) to lactic acid (found in milk). If you think about the differing acid levels of these two beverages, it will help you remember what this fermentation does to your wine — it reduces acid levels slightly and improves the fresh taste of wines. It can also give the wine just a hint of a sparkle — not bubbly like champagne, but not quite as still as ordinary wines. This third fermentation doesn't happen all the time, but we always consider ourselves lucky when it does!

Q. I'm concerned about making wines from flowers and herbs because I know some of them are poisonous. You mention oleander and lily of the valley (see page 74). Are there other plants that I should avoid?

A. Yes. The area of greatest concern is probably flowers. Since most people use flowers only for decoration, written information about them doesn't usually say whether they are toxic in food or beverages. Here are some plants to avoid ingesting: acacia, alder, aquilegia, azalea, belladonna, black nightshade, bluebell, buttercup, carnation, chrysanthemum, columbine, Christmas rose (hellebore), clematis, cotoneaster, crocus, cyclamen, daffodil, dahlia, delphinium, foxglove, geranium, hemlock, henbane, holly, honeysuckle berries, laurel, lilac, lobelia, lupins, marsh marigold, meadow rue, mistletoe, monkshood, peony, poppy, rhododendron, rhubarb leaves, and sweet pea. There are undoubtedly others, so, as we said earlier, a good rule of thumb is: if you're not sure, don't use it. In addition to these plants, avoid fungi of any kind, even mushrooms, and be sure to check an herb encyclopedia before you make herbal wines; the properties of herbs are usually well documented.

Q. You mention blending wines to get the flavors you want. Are there some rules of thumb for blending wines?

A. What most winemakers strive for when they create wine is a finished product that is *balanced*: It's neither thick and syrupy nor thin and bodiless; it's neither too intense in flavor nor too dull; it's neither too sweet nor so dry that it makes you pucker; it isn't too acid or too harsh, but it has enough acid and tannin to give it zest. Even the color and bouquet should be pleasant, but not overdone. If you make an unbalanced wine, blending it with another wine that's weak in the opposite direction can greatly improve both wines — and you'll have twice as much good wine.

But blending only works when both wines are essentially good wines, wines that fall short by just a little. If you blend a bad or deteriorating wine with another wine, you'll just end up with a whole lot of bad wine.

Until you're more comfortable with blending wines, here are a few pointers. First, don't get crazy, looking for strange new combinations. Confine your blending to wines of the same type — red wines with red wines, whites with whites, etc.

Second, don't just dump two batches of wine together — if you hate the blend, you'll have 2 gallons of the stuff to contend with. Instead, blend a little at a time and keep track of the proportions — 1 part red wine A with 2 parts red wine B, for example. We sometimes use shot glasses as a measure and experiment until we've found just the right blend — determined by lots of tasting, of course. Once we've decided on the best proportions, we blend the whole batch according to our taste tests, and return it to the fermentation vessels. Blended wines almost always re-ferment, but gently and for only a couple of days. When the bubbles stop rising, bottle the wine. It'll be even better after it's aged for at least 6 months.

Q. Can you give a quick list of mistakes I'm likely to make when I start making wine, so I can avoid them?

A. About the only mistakes in winemaking that can't be remedied by tasting, adjusting, or blending the wines result from contamination of some kind — that is, having something in the wine that alters the final flavor or results in spoilage. So right at the top of the list is cleanliness. Use clean equipment and pure, clean ingredients. Sterilize anything that comes into contact with your wine because it is likely to carry microorganisms. Don't use over-ripe or spoiling fruit. Make sure your water comes from a pure source. Use only non-reactive pots or kettles to cook or boil ingredients — glass, unchipped enamel, or stainless steel.

The second way that ingredients might be contaminated, resulting in off flavors if not downright spoilage, is if you inadvertently include crushed seeds, stems, or parts of the fruit that you wouldn't normally eat — crushed grape pips, the white inner rind of citrus fruits, the green fringe around flower blossoms, or the green parts of fruits.

Once you've made sure that your equipment and ingredients are uncontaminated, you'll need to make sure that they stay that way. Keep the first, aerobic fermentation under cover so no fruitflies contaminate the mixture. Use an airlock so that anaerobic fermentation takes place during the second fermentation to create enough alcohol to keep the wine from spoiling.

Keep careful records of everything you do and when you do it. And be patient. Very patient.

Q. What does it mean to let a wine "breathe"?

A. Some winetasters have found that certain wines, especially red ones, improve if the bottle is opened a half hour or so before the wine is served. That allows any gasses that may have collected in the bottle to dissipate. White wines, which are usually fresher tasting than red ones, do not usually need to breathe.

Q. How long can you keep an opened bottle of wine?

A. For really best quality, wine should be consumed shortly after it's opened. Oxidation begins very soon, especially in wines that aren't very acid. For that reason, some winemakers avoid bottling their wines in large containers, unless they are intended for party use where a large number of people are likely to be present. We've stored white wines in the refrigerator for a day or two with little bad effect, but since red wines are most often served at room temperature, we try to avoid having partial bottles of the reds. They can be stored in the refrigerator, of course, but they need to warm up to room temperature before they develop their full flavor. We think repeated chilling and warming has a negative effect on the flavor of red wine.

Glossary of Winemaking Terms

*N*ot all the terms in this glossary will be found elsewhere in this book; they have been included here to give the reader more comprehensive coverage of the subject of winemaking.

Aerobic fermentation: Fermentation in the presence of air. Aerobic fermentation usually occurs at the beginning of the fermentation process, before the wine is transferred to an airlocked vessel, where *anaerobic fermentation* (see below) will take place. Aerobic fermentation is usually a short, vigorous fermentation.

After-dinner wines: Wines such as port, muscatel, or Malaga, often fortified, but always sweet, consumed after a meal is completed.

Aging: Holding the wine in an airlocked vessel or bottle for 6 months to a number of years in order to allow time for changes that occur after fermentation that make the wine mellower and more pleasing to drink.

Alcohol: Ethyl alcohol is the component in wine that acts as a preservative and an intoxicant. About half the weight of the sugar in the must will be converted to alcohol.

Anaerobic fermentation: This fermentation, in the absence of air, occurs in the fermentation vessel once an airlock has been affixed. Any air that was present in the bottle is quickly expelled through the airlock and replaced with carbon dioxide, a by-product of the fermentation process. Anaerobic fermentation is usually a long fermentation and the one in which almost all of the alcohol in a wine is produced.

Antioxidant: A substance that prevents excess oxidation in wine — usually ascorbic acid — added to wine at the time it's bottled. Also called a *stabilizer*. A good test to see if you need to add ascorbic acid when you bottle your wine is to pour some wine into a glass and let it sit for 24 hours. If it turns brown, add 1/2 to 1 teaspoon of powdered ascorbic acid to a gallon of wine before bottling.

Apéritif: Apéritif wines are usually dry, high-alcohol wines served before a meal as an appetizer.

Atmosphere: Often used as a measure of the pressure created inside the bottle of a sparkling wine like champagne. An atmosphere is about fourteen pounds per square inch, and some champagnes are under six to seven atmospheres of pressure. That's why you need special bottles for sparkling wines.

Bacteria: Microorganisms that can be found in wines or on equipment that is not sterilized. Bacteria are usually responsible for wine spoilage or for wine turning to vinegar. You can usually tell if your wine is spoiled by bacteria because it will develop unpleasant (or vinegar) odors, and often a scum will form on top of a finished wine, indicating that oxidation has taken place.

Balance: A wine is said to be balanced when the components of the wine, including alcohol content, acidity, and residual sugar, as well as the flavor components of the wine, are in harmony with each other.

Body: The texture or fullness of a wine, the way it feels in your mouth. Body probably results from the alcohol and glycerine content — not the sweetness — of the wine.

Bouquet: A complex, rich smell that develops in wines as they age. Winetasters usually pick up a stemmed glass of wine, swirl it around gently, and smell the wine before they taste it. After sipping and swallowing a wine, if you breathe out gently through your nose with your mouth closed, you'll enjoy a second aspect of a wine's bouquet.

Campden tablet: Each containing about 7 grains of potassium metabisulfate, Campden tablets are dissolved in must or wine, where they release sulfur dioxide, which acts as a sterilant and antioxidant. (See pages 13–14 and 132–133.)

Cap: A term used in two ways by winemakers. The first, most obvious definition involves sealing the bottles against outside air once fermentation is complete. Those winemakers who cap their wine usually use a capping machine to apply the caps. Most country winemakers prefer corks, which can be applied with ease. The second use of the term refers to the somewhat firm layer of grapes or other solids that rises to the surface of the must during the primary fermentation. Some recipes call for "punching a hole in the cap" to admit oxygen. The cap, as well as any sediment in the bottom of the fermentation vessel, is left behind at the first racking.

Capsule: The foil or plastic sleeve placed over the cork and neck of a wine bottle to make a secure closure and improve the appearance of the bottle.

Clarifying: The process by which the suspended particles in a wine are removed — including filtration, racking, and *fining* (see below).

Clarity: A term used to describe the transparency or clearness of a wine. Wine should be clear and sparkling, not cloudy.

Color: A broad term used to describe the hue of the wine. Wines vary from nearly colorless white wines to deep burgundy red wines with golden, pink, and all the shades of red in between. Clarity and color are part of the visual experience of enjoying wines.

Concentrates: Juices prepared commercially by removing water. In some cases, concentrates are mixtures of juices from different varieties of grapes or blends of fruit juices. Others are pure juices of one variety or kind of fruit. Be sure to read the list of ingredients on the label before using them in your wines. Concentrates packaged specifically for winemaking will tell you on the label how much wine results from that quantity of concentrate. Usually water is added even to regular-strength juices in winemaking, because they are too intensely flavored and too expensive to use in large quantities of wine. Concentrates need even more additional water.

Dessert wines: Served with desserts, these wines are usually sweet and have a high alcohol content. Fortified wines (often served with dessert) have added alcohol to balance the alcohol with the sweetness. (See *fortification*.)

Dry: The term used by winetasters to describe a wine with little residual sugar. A dry wine causes the slight puckering of the mouth that winetasters use as a criterion for measuring sweetness. Wines may be brut (very dry), dry, semi-dry, semi-sweet, or sweet, depending on the amount of sugar left in the wine once the fermentation is complete. Most dry wines have about 1 percent residual sugar, but the percentage difference between sweet and dry is slight.

Energizer: Another name for a yeast nutrient, usually containing phosphates plus vitamin B_1 (thiamine).

Enzymes: Organic compounds that make possible chemical reactions that would fail to occur if they were not present. In winemaking, enzymes are important in several chemical reactions that take place during the fermentation process. You don't have to add them, however, as they are present in the ingredients you use. (See *pectic enzyme*.)

Fermentation: The process by which yeast turns sugar into alcohol and carbon dioxide.

Fermentation lock: A device used by winemakers to prevent air from entering the fermentation vessel while allowing carbon dioxide to escape. Also called an *airlock* or a *fermentation trap*.

Filtration: The process of running wine through paper or other material to physically remove suspended materials.

Fining: A term used to describe a process of clarifying wine by removing the sediments and other agents that keep it from having a brilliant, sparkling appearance. (See page 133.)

Fixed acids: Acids generally present in grapes and other fruits — such as malic, tartaric, citric, tannic, and phosphoric acids. They are called *fixed* because they are nonvolatile.

Flocculation: Name given to the process of coalescence and settling of yeast cells into a firm deposit.

Fortification: The process of adding distilled spirits to a finished wine in order to increase its alcohol content, keeping qualities, or flavor.

Hydrometer: A device used to measure *specific gravity* (see below) in order to determine alcohol content or potential alcohol content of wine. Using a hydrometer allows the winemaker to adjust the amount of sugar in the must for greater control of the sweetness or dryness of the wine. Hydrometers are available from many winemaking-equipment suppliers and come with complete instructions for their use. (See pages 143–144.)

Lees: Sediment made up of precipitated solids and dead yeast cells that collect in the bottom of a fermentation vessel in wine-making. Occasionally, if you're careless about racking or if you bottle just a little too soon, you may also find lees in your bottled wines.

Mead: Any wine whose primary energy source (sugar) and flavor are derived from honey. Honey wines need added yeast nutrients to complete the fermentation process, since these are not present in sufficient quantities in the honey itself.

Melomel: Any wine based on honey whose primary flavor is derived from fruit.

Metabisulfite: Sodium or potassium metabisulfite releases sulfur dioxide as a sterilant or antioxidant when added to must or wine in the form of crystals or a Campden tablet.

Metheglin: Any wine based on honey whose primary flavor is derived from herbs or spices.

Must: The term used to describe wine in its beginning stages, when there are large fruit particles, yeast, and juice present in the mixture.

Mycoderma: A spoilage organism that consumes alcohol and in the process impairs the flavor of the wine.

Nose: The aroma or bouquet of a wine, the smell that is released when the wine is swirled around in a wineglass or warmed by the heat of the sipper's hand. A good "nose" is part of the enjoyment in wine drinking.

Palate: A term often used by winetasters to describe the taste experience of a wine.

Pectic enzyme: An enzyme often added to wine to digest the pectin in the solution. Winemakers use pectic enzyme to convert pectins to sugars, because otherwise these waxy substances stay suspended in the wine and cause cloudiness.

Pectin: A substance present in some fruit, particularly underripe fruit, that is responsible for the jelling action in jams and jellies. In wines it stays suspended and causes cloudiness. It can be eliminated by pectic enzyme.

pH: This term is used to describe the relative acidity of a solution. Since some acidity is desirable in wine, a pH below 7 is wanted; a pH above 7 (neutral) indicates a basic solution.

Press: In this book, a device for forcing juice out of fruit pulp (see pages 149–150).

Primary fermentation: Occurs in the presence of air and is also called *first fermentation* or *rapid fermentation*. The most energetic of the fermentation processes, the primary fermentation quickly converts sugars to alcohol and carbon dioxide, causing a rapid drop in *specific gravity* (see page 163) in the solution. The length of and ideal conditions for the primary fermentation depend on the kind of wine that's being made. (See *aerobic fermentation*.)

Proof: A term used to describe the alcohol content of wines and spirits. It is equal to twice the percentage of alcohol in the solution, hence a wine with 10 percent alcohol is a 20-proof wine.

Racking: The name given to the process of syphoning cleared wine from a fermentation vessel into a clean container. Racking gives wine its clarity, as fruit solids, impurities, and yeast residue are left behind in the sediment.

Residual sugar: The amount of sugar left in the wine after the fermentation is complete. In wines, fermentation stops either when all of the available sugar has been used up, or when the concentration of alcohol reaches a point at which further yeast growth is inhibited. The residual sugar that remains gives the wine its sweetness.

Rosé: A pink wine, usually made by allowing only part of the first fermentation to take place with the skins of red or purple grapes in the must. The skins are removed before they impart their full color to the wine.

Secondary fermentation: The slower, second fermentation, which takes place in the absence of air, creating more alcohol as the yeast grows. (See *anaerobic fermentation.*)

Specific gravity: A term used to describe the density of a solution. When the wine has not yet begun the fermentation process, the specific gravity is high due to the suspended sugar particles in the must. As the wine ferments, the sugar is converted to alcohol and carbon dioxide, and the specific gravity of the solution lowers. Specific gravity can be measured with a *hydrometer* (see above), a device many winemakers use to determine the alcohol or potential alcohol content of wine.

Stabilizer: A substance added to wine, such as ascorbic acid or potassium sorbate, that prevents oxidation. (See *antioxidant.*)

Starter-culture: In winemaking, a strongly fermenting culture made from juice, yeast, and yeast nutrient, which is added to the other wine ingredients to start the fermentation process. (See page 15.)

Sterilants: Chemicals, such as Campden tablets, used to inhibit wild yeast and bacteria that may cause spoilage in wines. Also, substances that perform the same function on equipment, such as household bleach.

Stuck fermentation: Term used to describe a fermentation that stops without having converted all the available sugar to alcohol, usually due to some imbalance in the winemaking ingredients. (See page 146 for more information.)

Sulfites: Sulfur residue left over from the chemical reaction that produces sulfur dioxide when a Campden tablet is added to wine, for example. Usually harmless in the minute quantities in which it occurs in wine, but may cause allergic reactions in some people. (See pages 144–145.)

Sulfur dioxide: A gas released by Campden tablets and other metabisulfites that sterilizes and prevents oxidation in must and wine; the gas dissipates, but the chemical reaction produces sulfur salts, or sulfites, which remain in the wine.

Sweet wine: Any wine that has enough residual sugar — usually more than 1 percent — to give it a sweet taste. (See *dry*.)

Table wine: A wine that is served with meals. It may cleanse the palate, stimulate the appetite, and provide subtle contrasts with the food flavors. Any wine that helps accomplish these things — in short, any wine whose flavor, bouquet, and consistency pleases you — may be served with food. Usually white wines are served with light-colored meat or fish, rosés with chicken or other poultry dishes, and red wines with red meats, such as steak or roast beef, but these choices represent popular preferences only, not hard-and-fast rules.

Tannin: An astringent substance found in grape pips and stems, oak leaves, and tea. Needed in small quantities to improve the keeping quality of wines and to provide balance. (See pages 146–147.)

Topping up *or* topping off: The addition of a sugar-and-water syrup (see pages 139–140) or wine from a reserve supply to fermentation vessels to keep the container full. The process reduces the possibility of oxidation. Also used at the bottling stage to completely fill a bottle.

Yeast nutrients: The substances that yeasts must have in their "diets" so that they remain healthy and growing. Some country-wine recipes, especially for some of the honey-based wines, are deficient in naturally occurring yeast nutrients, so these must be added in order for the yeast to continue to grow and produce alcohol from the sugars present in the must.

Mail-Order Sources
for Winemaking Supplies

Aetna Wine Supplies
708 Rainier Avenue South
Seattle, WA 98118

Henry Field Seed and Nursery Co.
415 North Burnett Street
Shenandoah, IA 51602

Gurney Seed and Nursery Co.
110 Capitol Street
Yankton, SD 57079

E.S. Kraus
P.O. Box 451
Nevada, MO 64772

Milan Laboratory
57 Spring Street
New York, NY 10012

Nichols Garden Nursery
1190 North Pacific Highway
Albany, OR 97321

Semplex of USA
Box 12276
Minneapolis, MN 55142

The Winemaker's Shop
Bully Hill, RFD #2
Hammondsport, NY 14840

Wines, Inc.
1340 Home Avenue
Akron, OH 44310

Index

Figures in **boldface** indicate illustrations.

Sterilants, 13; definition of, 163
Storing: cellaring, 10; opened bottles, 156; rack, storing, 9, **9**
Straining, 152
Strawberry kiwi salad, 96
Strawberry melomel, 62
Strawberry wine, 30; fruit salad, 95; sweet wild-strawberry dessert, 30
Strawberry wine punch, 81
Stuck fermentation, 6, 164
Stuck wine, 146
Sugar, 148; residual, 163
Sulfite, 16, 144–45; definition of, 164
Sulfur dioxide, definition of, 164
Supplies, 11–14. *See also* Equipment; mail order sources, 166

T

Tangerine melomel, 61
Tannin, 5, 14, 146; definition of, 164; grape, 14; oak leaves as, 14; raisins as, 14, 142; tea as, 14
Tarragon metheglin, 68
Thyme metheglin, lemon, 69
Thyme wine, lemon, 75
Titration, 132
Topping up/off, definition of, 164
Turkey, 105–7

V

Vinegar, 5, 120–30; aromatic, 127; cider, 126–37; fiesta, 129; raspberry, 128; savory salad, 129; storing, 121; wine, 125–26
Vinegar cask, 121–23
Vinegar fly, 5
Vinello, 123

W

Water, 144, 148
Wheat wine, sweet, 49
Wine: aging, 140; blending, 154–55; breathing, 156; cooking with, 92–119; spoiled wine, 144; storing, 142; sweet, 134, 164; table, 164
Wine bottles, 8, **9.** *See also* Bottling; Jug wines; reusing, 138
Wine coolers, 80–91. *See also specific type;* basic, 87
Wine custard, 115
Wine punches, 80–91. *See also specific type;* lafayette, 86; passionate fruit, 82; tropical, 81, 90
Wine sauce: roast leg of lamb with, 102; sirloin steak with, 100
Wine terminology, 136–37
Winemaking: and refined sugar, 148; history of, 3–4; legal requirements, 2; mistakes, 155–56
Wormwood, 74

Y

Yams, Caribbean, 98
Yeast, 52, 134–35; champagne, 12, 56; commercial, 12; port yeast, 12
Yeast nutrient, 13, 50, 52, 65, 141; definition of, 165
Yeast starter-culture, 15, 56, 147

Z

Zabaglione, 115
Zinger pizza, vegetable, 94